Garden Styles

TIPS AND IDEAS FOR GARDENS WITH A DISTINCTIVE CHARACTER

FIEKE HOOGVELT

INTRODUCTION BY RICHARD ROSENFELD

REBO
PRODUCTIONS

© 1995 Zuid Boekprodukties, Lisse
© 1996 Published by Rebo Productions Ltd
Text: Fieke Hoogvelt
Translation: Guy Shipton for First Edition Translations Ltd, Great Britain
Jacket design and layout: Ton Wienbelt, The Netherlands
Photo editing: TextCase, The Netherlands
Production: TextCase, The Netherlands
Typesetting: M. Gregori for First Edition Translations Ltd, Great Britain

ISBN 1 901094 31 6

Contents

Introduction

Gardening is a bit like cookery. You come up with brand new recipes and discover they've been done before - in Turkey in the 14th century. And jolly good they were. The main difference between the present and the past though, is that gardens now tend to be uniformly smaller while the range of plants is so much greater. And to add to the irony, our dreams are that much bigger, and more ambitious, because we're more aware, more educated, not just of what the great the ancient gardeners did, but of what went on abroad. So the big question is, not just which style do we want for the garden, but how can we pack it all in? And where on earth do we start? Garden Styles holds back the reigns, and makes us get our hands dirty. Take a look at the soil. I remember getting to grips with my first garden. A 3-acre site in the Cotswolds. In summer the soil was like an elephant's back. Barnacled, crusty, lumpy and impervious. Unless it rained for seven days running, the water raced off into a weed-filled, 3m (1ft) ditch. With dreams spinning round in my head of visits to Cang Lang Ting in China, which has a hill not a pond in the centre, and a weekend at the Corsi-Salviati in Italy, which has all the romantic ingredients, including a large fake castle, and Nishat Bagh in India, one of the Mogul Lake Dal gardens, I had to contend with this. Soil that was harder than leather. You would not expect Venus to rise out of glue; why should roses perform in concrete? When books and TV programmes talk about tipping on manure and compost, they mean it. I dumped in manure from the stables (where they trained a Derby winner), mushroom compost, anything from round the cow sheds, and best of all plenty of chicken mess. If you're lucky enough to live by a zoo, come to a private arrangement. There's even a company in England that sells tubs of what they call zoo poo; concentrated, composted elephant manure. Apparently it's very successful. And I dug and I dug and I dug. And I left the ground all open and lumpy, right through winter, in quite an amazing mess, and everyone who walked through the village looked away, like it was something that should not be seen, and the at the end of the next spring I dug again and raked it over, and the soil was actually crumbly. Not so that anyone would notice. But I did. It sifted like sand through my fingers. I'd smashed my concrete foe. And that, I later learnt, was just the start of the start. But you remember it, years later, when you've forgotten everything else. Getting to grips with a garden stays deep inside your head. So does laying the grass. As Fieke Hoogvelt says, the history of grass goes back 2,000 years. Only the Romans sensibly used canomile. And later generations used daisies, violets, periwinkle and primroses, which today we'd call very New Age, a kind of manicured field with wild flowers. And there's no reason why we should not revert to that. The grass lawn is just a 19th-century invention. Garden Styles is exactly the kind of book every gardener should read. It constantly puts the now in a wider perspective, and suggests how everything can be reinvented and fine tuned. The book sparks new ideas. Turf seats turf beds, a place to sleep in the summer? Why not? It's as if garden design is in our collective genes. The same ideas keep coming around but in ingeniously modified ways. All you have to decide is, which vision shall I plant up?

Richard Rosenfeld, East Sussex, 1996

The origins of the most important garden styles

In the Bible, we are told that God created heaven and earth and all the things upon it. Lastly, He created man. "The Lord God planted a garden eastward in Eden."

"And out of the ground made the Lord God to grow every tree that is pleasant to the sight, and good for food." The rivers Euphrates and Tigris flowed through the garden, where God put the first people. Adam was to tend and maintain this garden. In fact, he was the very first gardener.

In the middle of the 19th century it was felt that the informal garden should in effect be part of the landscape.

The enclosed garden

In distant antiquity, when nomadic tribes began to make more or less permanent settlements, wooded areas in the immediate vicinity were felled to build homes. The land which became available through this process was farmed and a few crops were cultivated on it.

Plants with thorns and spines were planted around these parcels of land to protect them from wild animals. People living in delta areas, such as the Netherlands, wove enclosures from willow withies which they called tun or tuin (modern Dutch for garden). Only later was the word tuin used to indicate the area which lay within the enclosure. This word can be found in many languages. In English an area surrounded by walls and ditches was called a "town", while in German an enclosed or hedged area was called Zaun.

Ancient gardening history

Depictions of the oldest gardens have been found in Egyptian pyramids. It is clear that these were for functional purposes – places where fruit-bearing trees, bushes, and plants such as dates, figs, and vines were grouped around a pond or alongside an irrigation canal.

5

Fish swam in the ponds where the sacred lotus and papyrus grew. For practicality's sake these waterworks were rectilinear in shape. Out of this came the designs for all classic Mediterranean gardens constructed along axes and straight lines.

Egypt's influence stretched eastwards to Persia, where pleasure gardens were called *pairidaeza*, from which comes the word "paradise". The layout of the Persian garden was of importance to the development of subsequent garden styles.

Water is of essential importance in Persia and in other subtropical regions. There was always a supply of water in the garden: either from a well or irrigation canals. The well stood in the centre of the garden surrounded by a paved area, from each side of which emanated four paths. The paths split the garden into quarters which exemplified the four divisions of the universe. Useful produce was grown in each quarter, including peaches, figs, dates, grapes, and many medicinal herbs. Since these ancient peoples had a great reverence for trees, many cypresses, which were symbolic of eternity, and other trees were planted around the edge of such gardens. On hillier ground it was possible to irrigate gardens, having them laid throughout with water channels. These channels were often widened in the centre of the garden to form a pond. Later, the beds and water began to be put to decorative use by the inclusion of many plants, such as bulbs, native to Persia. The paths alongside the waterways were decorated with

tiles and mosaic work. Water splashed over the little dams and fountains, spurting water into the air. Arbours were first employed to support vines. Later on they became more decorative and served as shelter from the sun. Although many decorative features were added to these gardens, the original rigid layout was maintained. Wells and channels (or irrigation systems) continually reappeared throughout the whole civilized world.

The original, Persian garden plan evolved into the patio seen in the courtyards of Italian and Spanish homes. In the centre of the patio was a pond, fountain, or well, and grouped around this were plants in pots or tubs. In the Netherlands a similar garden design can be seen in old cottage gardens fronting the house. In this adaptation there is often no well in the centre since the climate does not create much need for extra water. Instead of a well, there might be a circular flower-bed, a sundial, or a car tyre filled with flowers.

The Greeks and the Romans   Little is known about Greek gardens. The educated Greek did no manual work, but rather exerted himself mentally. The Greeks were nature-lovers, nonetheless. In Homer's *Odyssey* we read descriptions of nature which speak of beautiful lands and the various plants growing there such as pomegranates, figs, olive trees, and vines. We also know that medicinal and even kitchen herbs were cultivated. Yet although the Greeks revered trees and even planted them in sacred

7

A prerequisite for sun-dials is that they should receive sunlight all day

groves, they did not have a particularly edifying gardening culture. They were sculptors and architects, educated Greeks spending their time in sporting activities, military strategy, religious worship, and debate. The rooms of a Greek house were built around a courtyard. An arcade, or stoa, ran along the edge of this courtyard.

The Romans were more practical and down-to-earth. These were the conquerors of the world. They subjected people to their rule including the Etruscans, Greeks, and those in the Middle East – and learned how to master their skills. This happened in such a way that it seemed as though these skills had come from their own discoveries. The Romans were wealthy and enjoyed outdoing each other. Not only were temples, theatres, and bath-houses built but the ordinary citizen's home was also greatly transformed. Architecture, which had been borrowed from the Greeks, was improved upon by using the arch which had come from the Etruscans. Bigger rooms could be built as a result.

Nature had to be mastered as well as architecture. Pliny the Younger tells us in his writings how villa gardens looked at the time. Several attempts have been made to reconstruct these gardens, but the results all look quite different. For example, a reconstruction from 1860 makes one think of the English countryside, while a yet earlier, French one makes one think more about the monumental grandeur of Versailles. Therefore, these reconstructions give us an impression of

One of the more attractive properties of an urn is that its lid prevents it from being filled with plants

the people who made them and the times in which they lived, and certainly not of Roman gardens as they actually were.

It is known with certainty that town houses had courtyards where pot plants and flowers could be seen next to a pond. Topiary became fashionable for the wealthy. Status and power had to be expressed in topiary designs, ranging from a hunting scene to the owner's name. The Roman ornamental-garden slave, the *toparius*, was in charge of the topiary.

Medieval gardens At the time of the fall of the Roman Empire the whole of Europe was plunged into chaos. Many battles were waged and there was no time for building or gardening artistry. Homes were strengthened into fortresses and castles. Castles were encircled by a double row of embankments and ditches. Within the castle walls there was always a kitchen garden where alongside cabbage, carrots, beans, onions, and radishes there were also the cultivated herbs for culinary use, and even fruit such as strawberries and melons. The rest of the area, around which were situated the stables, store-houses, and work sheds, was an earthen surface which was either rock solid or else became a great quagmire of mud.

This remained the situation until more wagons began to be used, generally following the same tracks which were afterwards paved. This paved road evolved into a driveway planted with trees. The

earthen central area was then sown with grass seed to keep down weeds and prevent dust from blowing about. A lime tree was always placed next to the well or spring as protection against storms and under it courting lovers would sit.

Only after 1600, when Europe had become more stable, were orchards planted outside the embankments and ditches and flowers added to the inner court (amongst the grass).

Spiritual life flourished greatly in the Middle Ages. Monks were extremely learned and knew a great deal about herbal remedies. The inner court of the monastery was used for the cultivation of medicinal herbs and flowers where, originally, grass had been sown. Two paths crossed this inner garden bisecting each other and thus dividing the garden into four parts. Each individual bed was often given a border of box, Buxus, which was used on Palm Sunday.

Townspeople became so prosperous that they also laid out gardens. They regularly incorporated a decorative element in the centre. However tiny these parcels of land might have been, there was always a wall surrounding them. Decorative plants were grown, as well as vegetables and herbs. The preference was for roses and lilies, and, as regards fruit trees, apples, pears, or figs were often planted. A bench of built-up soil covered in turf was considered appropriate for relaxation in the garden, and often enough it was covered with flowers. There are many depictions of the Virgin Mary and the infant Jesus sitting on

One of the most rewarding garden plants is Alchemilla mollis.*, for centuries a favourite in gardens of all styles. Its great clumps of yellow flowers are useful in filling up borders or providing their edging. The plant becomes bushier when 'pruned back' after its first flowering and may even flower a second time.*

such benches, which explains why these gardens were called Mary Gardens.

Since not all gardens had high walls, painted fences and lattice-work (trellised) arbours were also employed. Usually, these were heavily grown over.

An arbour, when connected to the house, was often used as a second living room or bedroom.

Later on, people were no longer content with just one small garden, and larger gardens started to be divided up into smaller ones, each for a distinct purpose.

The Renaissance   The medieval monastic orders collapsed during the sixteenth century. Papal and imperial influences over much of the population were lost. A person no longer wished to be simply a part of the masses, but wanted to be seen as a free, independent individual. By travelling widely, people came into contact with other cultures and as a consequence of this broadened outlook and their almost unbounded curiosity many discoveries were made. The spirit of the times was a preoccupation with earthly matters.

Through trading, wealthy Italians amassed gold, silver, silks, and art objects. Families such as the Borgias and Medici built huge palaces and villas with which they outstripped each other in terms of beauty and riches.

The early Renaissance garden in Italy was almost always composed of several terraces and divided up into a number of quadrangles. No attention was paid to the nature of the terrain or the environment. Every quadrangle had its own theme: ornamental, herb garden, orchard or vineyard, and water. There was always a decorative feature in the middle of the quadrangle, a statue or group of statues, or a fountain, while the beds themselves were bordered with hedges or lined with aisles of dense foliage. The quadrangles were linked to each other by identical paths or avenues of no particular connection with the villa. The whole was surrounded, sometimes in a quadrangular form as well, by *boscos*: trees or shrubs planted in a set pattern.

Renaissance gardens can be recognized by their use of water and sculpture. They were gardens intended for pleasure and diversion. Permanent elements included geometrically shaped beds, little trees planted in the beds, a lawn, mazes, and topiary.

In the Netherlands, at that time made up of the present-day Netherlands and Belgium, the Renaissance garden was strongly influenced by Jan Vredeman de Vries. He fell under the influence of Italy, although he had never been there. Dutch gardens were smaller in layout. The shape was rectangular, the garden being divided lengthways into equal halves with the central axis bisecting the house. The two halves were further split into several, quadrangular garden sections. The garden was enclosed by a wall, a belt of trees, or a

A fence made from interwoven willow withies lends extra charm to present-day gardens.

system of water channels. Garden features often included a maze, a pergola, a covered arbour, a trellis for training fruit trees, small fruit trees, box hedging, and low-lying ornamental plants such as thyme, carnations, and camomile. Water played a lesser role, although fountains and trick jets of water did appear now and then. There were few garden statues, although the sundial was a standard component of Dutch Renaissance gardens.

A parterre de broderie *at Het Loo Palace in the Netherlands.*

The baroque
The small communities, so typical of the Renaissance, grew larger in the baroque period, and rationalism and individuality reigned supreme. Royal houses increased their power; not only in terms of state affairs, but also in religious and artistic matters. They exhibited their power with great pomp and circumstance. This change in perspective also had an influence on the arts. More depth was seen in the subject matter of paintings, singing developed into the rondo in music, which in the Renaissance was still performed with only a few instruments. Sonatas and symphonies began to evolve.

Gardens in the Renaissance were concerned with refinement in seclusion, whereas the baroque impressed on the viewer the magnificence of the surroundings. The baroque garden's apogee was reached at Versailles. Many baroque gardens were laid out in France and Germany. In the Netherlands, where no great, central authority existed, gardens remained much smaller.

In the early baroque, colour was added to the parterres de broderie by using coloured pebbles.

Monumental garden design was characteristic of this period in which the central axis, aligned with the chief room of a building, was very strongly accentuated. In this way, house and garden became a single entity. The enclosed quadrangles of the Renaissance evolved into open rectangles with a ratio of 3:5. Decorative features no longer stood in the centre of a parterre, but at the intersection of the axes. A long view was achieved by laying out large and small areas alternately along the length of the main axis. In France, Louis XIV's gardener, Le Nôtre, said: "I will not be restricted to a boundary for a view"; his avenues were not allowed to end before the horizon.

The spaces next to the main axis and between the transverse axes were filled with trees and coppices, each of which contained a charming surprise. Closer to the house were the *parterres de broderie*, often decorated with curling box borders. In the beginning of the baroque period, the areas lying between the box borders were filled with differently coloured pebbles, later with flowers; while flowers were also added as a border-surround to the parterres, known as a *plate bande*. Although these borders were completely filled in France, plants in the Netherlands were spaced out from one another in such flower-beds. Box disappeared from the parterres' straight borders.

Waterworks came to occupy an important place in gardens, alongside the requisite statuary, lattice-work tunnels and arbours, pergolas, urns, and vases.

The flowering plants are clearly separated in the strip which surrounds the parterre; a lattice-work tunnel is visible in the background.

14

Baroque turned imperceptibly into rococo. The chief characteristics of the baroque garden remained unaltered in this period, but the main axis of the garden was split into a fan of three or more equal axes. Because of this, the parterres could no longer remain rectangular. Ornamentation became very important, and the twisting box-border patterns became much more complex. Winding paths were incorporated into the coppices which, until then, had been designed with paths radiating star-like from the centre.

When laying a path, pay special attention to its width. A path which seems to be too wide in an as yet unplanted garden will look precisely the right size when there are plants overhanging it.

The rise of the informal garden style

Once the people had shaken themselves loose of absolute monarchy after the French Revolution, and "liberty, equality, and fraternity" had started to take root for all citizens, gardening styles changed greatly. With advances in astronomy, man realized that he was but the tiniest fraction of the universe, and thus power was only a relative concept.

In 1750, Linnaeus wrote his *Species Plantarum*, in which all plants were systematically classified. In previous periods, people had only had a small number of plants at their disposal. Many plants were now being imported from other countries. People began to consider each individual plant as being of importance and no longer wanted to use plants simply as decorative material.

People came into contact with a completely different style through trading with China and Japan: the Chinese landscape style which had been established for centuries.

Statuary and large water gardens were the high point of baroque gardens.

More big cities began to appear. The city dwellers no longer had any contact with the countryside and began to glorify it.

All these new developments were incorporated within the new garden style. Country life was glamorized in the romantic garden. Hermitages were placed in the garden, while dark woodland, a splashing stream, crooked overhanging trees, and weeping trees forming a canopy over an urn were intended to conjure up all kinds of moods and images such as mournfulness, rusticity, and the picturesque. Country life was enhanced with rustic summer-houses which had to look like little farm houses, ideally with a bleating goat at the door.

The origin of the informal garden style

The Chinese were treating homes and gardens as separate entities a few thousand years before Christ. They took pleasure in the countryside and, at first, the garden was a little piece of nature; completely without straight lines and geometric shapes. Veneration of mountains was traditional and for this reason a "mountain" was always put into the garden near the house. Water, rocks, and trees were the most important ingredients in a garden. Emperor Wu, obsessed with the concept of immortality, sought out the Islands of Immortality, but never succeeded in finding them.

Legend tells how the immortals were carried on the backs of cranes. By digging lakes and placing islands in them the emperor hoped to attract the immortals to his garden. Carefully chosen boulders, a

Lavishly decorated urns were frequently used in baroque gardens.

symbol of the crane, were placed in the garden. These lake and island gardens were being made up to the nineteenth century. The pavilions and bridges, the *yang* element, brought structure into the garden. The garden's free form was the *yin* element. Because paths and fences wound their way through the garden, the vista was never the same from any two viewpoints.

Almost everything in the Chinese garden had a symbolic function. For example, there was the round gate of the moon, a circular opening in a wall or fence and a symbol of immortality. The chrysanthemum represented a long life, the plum tree hope and courage, and the pine tree a venerable old age.

Japan   Much of what we attribute to the Japanese was developed from the Chinese. The Japanese felt an intense love of nature. Gardeners made no use of foreign plants at all: nature was complete in itself. For this reason, gardens were created in which nature was precisely imitated. Looking closely at pine trees in a Japanese garden, one can see that they have in fact been pruned from top to bottom to make a natural shape. Pruning was an important feature of Japanese gardening artistry. It certainly was an art to conceal the artificiality and make the garden look like part of a perfectly harmonious, natural world. Stones, and the ways in which they were employed in the garden, had a meaning based on religious ideas.

The Japanese art of pruning is an utterly artificial technique used to give the garden a harmonious and natural appearance.

The fountain has been made excessively ornate, as a good "baroque sculpture" should be.

19

The lake and island gardens which reached their zenith in the seventeenth century appeared here too. "Dry gardens" were laid out in smaller meditation gardens next to temples. Waterfalls, river beds, sea, lakes, and islands were depicted using stones, sand, and gravel. Stones and rocks were employed in a special way: these materials had a symbolic significance. Gravel was raked into a wavy pattern making it look as if the tide had only just ebbed away.

Gardens for the tea ceremony also appeared in the seventeenth century. The path leading to the tea house was paved with stepping stones of different sizes, which compelled the contemplative visitor to analyse the symbolism behind them and uplifted the spirit. No flowers were planted in these gardens, but there were ferns, trees, and moss which evoked a feeling of serenity and timelessness. These gardens were lit by lanterns since they were also used at night for meditation.

Essential requirements for Japanese gardens are that they should remain attractive all year round, and should not be dependent on flowering plants. There are flowers, but only flawless examples of them. Potted chrysanthemums are only put outside when in flower. If no garden is available then a miniature garden or miniature trees (bonsai) can be grown in a dish.

Stones, water, a lantern, and bamboo – the ingredients of a Japanese garden par excellence.

The landscape style

A new style known as landscape was initiated in England during the romanticism of the eighteenth century. Sir Lancelot Brown was the

man of the moment. He was also known as Capability Brown because he always saw the "capabilities" for changing every garden into a landscape. The English countryside served as his example, especially that along the River Thames.

A number of features were introduced into the landscaped garden, which had to conform to certain fixed rules. For example, a pool took on the shape of a wide stretch of river. This water had to look like a river and the ends had to be invisibly hidden from sight. The house always had to be on higher ground than the lawns, which came right up to the house and had to dip somewhat in the middle. The clumps of trees on the lawn had to be planted on raised ground. The entire garden was enclosed by a ring of trees and bushes through which the major paths would lead. Broad-leaved trees were used, only occasionally conifers. The evergreens, box and holly, also appeared in these parks.

Brown's predecessor, William Kent, had allowed artistic devices such as little temples and classical architecture to be incorporated within the landscape. This was not permitted in the new landscape style. A bridge over the water or a single temple might just pass muster, but only if the garden was optically enlarged as a result. This style meticulously re-created nature.

Humphrey Repton, a successor to Brown, was less dogmatic. He reintroduced terraces, balustrades, and fountains next to houses and gave over plenty of space to flowers and flowering shrubs. Walled

In the informal garden, the growing requirements of plants are taken into account as far as possible.

gardens also reappeared in his designs. The pure landscape style began to disintegrate.

The rise of the town garden

Until the nineteenth century, a landscape-style garden was the exclusive preserve of rich landowners and for ordinary townsfolk there were only parks. In the nineteenth century, however, more and more people joined the middle classes. They lived in villas and terraced houses and very much wanted to learn how to lay out and maintain a garden. In 1826, the publisher John Claudius Loudon brought the first issue of *The Gardener's Magazine* onto the market. He embroidered Repton's principles, calling his new style "gardenesque". He emphasized the collection of new plants; giving advice on planting in kitchen and nursery gardens as well as working in greenhouses and with cold-frames. He attempted to consolidate the best elements from the garden styles which had existed up to that time. The point was that the garden had to look different from the surrounding landscape. Gardening clubs started to mushroom. Various garden styles were adopted in nineteenth-century gardens, including the informal garden. William Robinson felt that gardens should fit into the landscape. Flowers might be allowed to grow peacefully in the grass and why should a climber be forced to grow over an arbour when it could climb a tree? The use of hardy perennials was also promoted by him, but not in a narrow row of

Walls that are almost completely grown over belong to the cottage garden style too.

Left: A garden needing little tending – plenty of seating space and evergreen plants.

flowers planted beside the lawn and not in carpet beds. He had no prejudice against exotic plants as long as they were hardy.

The cottage style   The cottage style started up in the middle of the nineteenth century as a reaction against the plethora of styles at the time. A group of architects wanted to separate architecture from the past. They were looking for a new style which could feasibly be adapted in that period. Old handicrafts were recognized as having an important place in this, as well as the use of simple materials. The English country cottage served as an example. A unity was formed with rooms grouped around a central hallway, beamed ceilings replaced the ornamental style, and everything was complemented by the thatched roof and big chimneys.

The division of the cottage garden took its inspiration from the farmstead, where individual areas had a particular function (kitchen garden, work space, orchard, a place for manure, etc.). This was interpreted in the cottage garden by having, for example, a quiet, green area next to the study, a flower garden next to the living room, and a kitchen garden next to the kitchen. These independent little gardens were enclosed by small hedges and linked to each other in a co-ordinated system. Where paths crossed came the reappearance of statues, bird-baths, small fountains, and sundials. Gertrude Jekyll invented a border in which the flowering plants were all grouped

A garden with a welcoming approach.

together by colour, height, and flowering season. The hedge was used as a backdrop to these borders. The cottage style, and the landscape style in parks, continued to be interpreted up to 1940.

A contemporary garden with a tendency towards formal design.

Gardens today Nowadays, although individuals have less garden space, there is a choice of many more plants to put in the garden. There is much more knowledge about plants and a lot more interest in them, but little time (and few staff) to take care of them. For many the garden has become an extension of the home. The garden is a place for carrying out hobbies and life is lived in the garden. Conservatories, sun porches, and experimental greenhouses are really "in".

Formal elements have been adopted alongside features from the informal garden style. The tendency seems to be a desire to return to a natural ecosystem in which very little needs to be tackled. Wooded and "wild" gardens are often being laid out, containing plants adapted to soil and climatic conditions. Do not forget that gardens like this require maintenance too. You will definitely have to put in an appearance at regular intervals.

In the last few years, formal gardens have seen a come-back. Geometrically designed box borders, filled with roses or perennials, are to be seen everywhere. Cottage garden plants are being combined with the formal layout of gardens from previous centuries. No doubt, a name for this kind of garden style will be found in the next century.

Soil, the garden's foundation

This book pays appropriate attention to soil. The reason being that the condition of your soil determines the degree of success of your planting.

Left to its own devices, any patch of ground will obtain its own natural cover.

We are often impatient. Many of us want to start laying out and making changes to our gardens straight away, for there is nothing so dull as looking at an empty, brown space. Nonetheless, this empty, brown space is the ground on which it all has to happen; where your trees, shrubs, and other plants must be able to grow to their very best advantage. If we want to restrict the amount of maintenance and action on our part, we have to take the natural environment (including the soil) into account. Although "ground" and "soil" have differing meanings in garden literature, the difference is not always very clearly defined. For the sake of convenience, this chapter sticks to "soil". It is important for you to know what the positive and negative properties of your soil are, and how you can bring your influence to bear on this where it is necessary.

Soil type   Gardens are, for the most part, made up of soil – but what sort of soil? Driving through the country at large you will see continual changes in the topography. It might include low-lying reclaimed land, sandy hillocks, river flood-plains, coniferous forest, hilly or mountainous areas, broad-leaved woods, or sand dunes.

All these environments have different sorts of vegetation. This arises because the soil type, on which plants depend, varies according to the environment. We will firstly look at the most important soil types for our gardens.

Sand is weathered rock. It has a granular structure. Rain water quickly permeates down via the large pore spaces between the big granules, but poorer quality water can also be drawn up from below. The bigger the granules, the drier the soil. Sandy soil can always be recognized by the glittering particles scattered throughout it. Soil which is pure sand is poor in nutrients.

A natural coniferous wood growing on sandy soil.

Clay is also weathered rock, but is different in origin. Clay granules, or rather clay particles, are very much smaller than grains of sand. It is not surprising that water permeates down very slowly through these tiny pore spaces, and that clay soil can hold a lot of water and has poor drainage. Underground water permeates upwards only very gradually once a clay soil has dried out. A dry clay soil becomes as hard as a rock and begins to crack, and a wet clay soil becomes increasingly impervious to water when it rains because the pore spaces between the fine clay particles become waterlogged. Fortunately, there is a positive side to clay soil. It is naturally nutrient rich because the weathered rock from which it comes continues to weather. A lot of nutrients are released during this process.

Peat soil is, for the most part, made up of decomposed organic material. The soil can hold a large amount of water and yet still permit drainage. Peat soil which lies high above the water table will continue decomposing and settling. Plants grow quickly but less strongly in this soil's natural humus. Problems arise with peat soil where there is too much water.

Sandy clay is a mixture of fine sand and clay. These two components determine this soil's properties. Sandy clay is usually fertile, easy to work, and moisture retentive, and enables good root growth.

Loamy soil is very like sandy clay, and is also fertile and easy to work.

This summary of the most prevalent soil types may not have been cheering news to your ears since precise definitions of soil characteristics, especially the negative ones, clearly bring problems to your attention. Fortunately, all will usually go well in practice, for the difficult soil types only rarely appear in their pure form.

Soil structure The soil's composition, its structure, depends on the various components of the soil such as soil particles, water, and air; *and* the behaviour of those components when related to each other. Soil life, the amount of organic material, and also the chemical properties of the soil are perpetual influences on its structure.

For example, soil can be said to have a poor structure when many puddles of water remain on the surface for a long time after a shower. The soil either has poor permeability or else there is a disruptive layer of soil beneath the surface. In sandy soils this impermeable layer could be an iron-pan. In peat soils a water-soaked layer of clay can block the link between upper and lower soil levels. The problem in new town developments can be that clay soil has been driven over and flattened completely, and a layer of garden soil has simply been placed on top of this. And what about the layer of cement where the cement-mixers were standing?

There is also something wrong with the structure if soil starts to blow away when there are gusts of wind. It could be that the soil is not taking up any water from below after a dry spell or that it is forming a hard, crusty surface.

It is clear that bothersome layers need to be broken through. This is very often not at all easy to achieve, and entails work in any case. However, many other problems can be solved by constantly adding quantities of humus.

Humus Everything which is left over after the decomposition of vegetation and animals (including the animal itself as well as its excreta) is known as humus. This is organic material. Plant and animal remains – like leaves, stems, wood, sawdust, roots, dead animals, and smaller organisms – will produce a dark brown compost after a slow "breaking down" or conversion process. All kinds of other materials which plants need in order to survive are also released by this. This

TIP

An impervious layer of soil can be broken through by using a soil drill to make a hole 6cm (2in) in diameter every 3m (10ft). Fill the hole with gravel to a maximum level of 25cm (10in) below the surface. Fill the upper 25cm (10in) with garden soil. Excess water can then drain away underground via the bore holes.

organic material makes up the soil's food supply. The soil forms a buffer in which this food supply is stored. All manner of unsightly little creatures, even smaller micro-organisms, and plants too, are fed by it. The good thing is that humus has a binding effect on sandy soils, which consequently improves moisture retention. Humus works wonders in clay soils too. It pushes the clay particles apart slightly which loosens it, enabling better drainage and making it easier to work. Since humus is dark in colour the soil also becomes darker which enables more absorption of the sun's warmth. This is advantageous to plant growth throughout the year.

One should be aware that the food supply is continually depleting and that after time it will be used up. This temporary humus must be replaced continually in order to maintain consistently beneficial effects in the soil.

Soil life varies according to soil depth

Mice, moles, voles, snails, earthworms, mites, insects and their larvae, fungi, and bacteria take care of cleaning up and thereby processing all vegetable and animal waste. This waste is their food. They break down organic material step by step. This material is reduced by chewing, gnawing, or shredding. The animals' droppings or waste products feed other, smaller creatures. Their waste products feed yet smaller organisms, and so on. At various points during all these stages, food becomes available to the plant. A glue-like substance is

Even today water remains an attractive garden feature.

produced during the on-going process, and soil particles become stuck to this, producing a crumbly soil. The soil organisms which feed chiefly on fresh organic material live in the uppermost soil layer. The smaller the organic waste particles become, the further this waste material descends below ground. You will have noticed how an earthworm will pull a dry leaf into the ground by its stem. This is particularly evident between paving stones. Fresh organic material never finds its *own* way deep below ground.

Air-dependent plants and animals are at work breaking down matter beneath ground level. From 5 to 20cm (2–8in) underground, where less oxygen is present, yet another group of organisms is active. These live off the waste products from the animals in the uppermost layer. From thereon downwards the soil becomes increasingly poor in oxygen.

Bacteria and fungi living in this oxygen-deficient environment die of shock when any digging brings them to the surface. By the same token, snails and scavenger beetles die at a depth of 20cm (8in) through lack of food and air. It is therefore recommended to keep the soil layers in place when performing digging work of all kinds. As far as manure, compost, and the like are concerned, these should be gently worked into the uppermost soil layer. Digging deeply can be necessary when laying out an ornamental garden, or when loosening the soil below to prepare a new border. Even then one should not mix up the soil layers.

Gravel and sea-shells prevent soil erosion by rain and combat weed growth.

These lines of bricks prevent soil from being washed away.

Soil, water, and air

Considering how many organisms are largely made up of water, it is only logical that water is essential to life on earth. Seventy to ninety percent of a plant is made up of water. Assisted by water a plant creates its own building materials. Water is needed to transport nutrients and maintain cell pressure. Plants allow water to evaporate and in this way prevent themselves from "overheating".

You have already seen how soil type can tell us about the soil's hydrology. Clay, humus-rich sandy soil, and peat soil can hold a lot of water. Poor sandy soil behaves more like a sieve.

Plant roots also require oxygen for their vital functions and this can be found in the pore spaces between soil granules, as long as these spaces are not saturated with water. Plant roots will die off if continually immersed in water, or if the water table suddenly rises, not through drowning but because of suffocation through lack of oxygen. By constantly adding humus we can try to make naturally dry soils moister, and clay soils a little drier.

Covering the soil

All soil develops cover naturally. Just place a flower-pot with potting compost outside for a while. Although you have not sown anything, all sorts of things will be growing in it after a few weeks. The germinated seeds will have come in the wind or via animals and will have found a suitable food source in which to grow. This is exactly what happens in the garden, be it of the ornamental or kitchen

On a sloping surface, without ground cover, soil is easily washed away.

Wood chips serve as excellent path cover in an informal setting. These wood chips do need regular replacement.

variety, or whatever. You can spend endless time weeding and hoeing, of course, but you will quickly come to the conclusion that this is an endless battle which you are doomed to lose. Furthermore, by taking away these "weeds" you are making the soil poorer. Meanwhile, haven't the weeds been taking nutrients from the soil too? Moreover, wind, sun, and rain have full reign over the bare ground. Heavy rain causes nutrients to be washed away, sunshine dries out the soil and influences its temperature, and wind blows away soil particles (erosion) and has an equally desiccating effect on the soil. The best you can do is to keep the ground completely covered. If you are using organic material as soil cover you will reduce weed growth *and* increase the nutrient level.

There are still more advantages to be had from "mulching": the soil will retain a constant moisture level while solar radiation, wind damage, and water erosion will be greatly reduced. The soil will also acquire a preferable crumbly, friable structure.

To make a mulch you can use leaves, peat, grass clippings, wood chips or bark, compost, and sawdust (not from painted materials or tropical hardwoods).

There are, however, a few disadvantages to a year-round mulch layer. The organic material attracts snails, mice, and moles. Therefore, move the mulch away from plants with large, succulent leaves such as *Hosta* (plantain lilies).

TIP

Nitrogen is needed to break down a layer of mulch which contains a lot of carbon (wood shavings, straw, and wood). If nitrogen is not mixed into the mulch layer, it will start to be extracted from the soil. Therefore the best idea is to add some nitrogen whilst preparing the mulch.

31

If you are gardening on wet soil, the mulch will keep the soil wetter and colder for longer, above all in the spring. The chances of late frost damage are greater than on drier ground.

Decorative plants can also be used as soil cover, particularly the ground-cover plants. People say that ground-cover plants stop weed growth, but I have noticed that various weeds do still come up through them regardless. This is especially annoying when the ground-cover plant that you have planted is a very thorny rose!

Many gardeners consider a mulch layer rather a messy sight and prefer to plant borders completely filled with shrubs and perennials. The evergreens amongst these plants keep the soil covered with their leaves. Let the leaves from plants which lose them in winter remain on the ground as soil cover for winter protection.

Suitable planting

Most of the plants in our gardens come from different parts of the world. One really should take a moment to consider that their origins include different soil types and being exposed to differing, climatological conditions. A plant will flourish if it has the ideal environment. A busy Lizzie, *Impatiens sultanii*, is not at all happy in a dry soil under the burning sun. A rose planted in a chalky soil will show its displeasure by producing yellow leaves. There will always be organisms lying in wait to attack and destroy the plant if its

Ground-cover plants growing tightly up against each other prevent weed growth, protect the soil, and keep the humus level constant.

Moss is a natural ground cover.

environment is not suitable. These can include mould and fungi, insects, and snails.

If you want a garden where you do not have to intervene too much, then, as far as possible, consider your choice of plants in relation to the soil's composition and the soil's nutrient level. Rhododendrons, blueberries (*Vaccinium*), and creeping willow (*Salix repens*) do well in moisture-retentive, humus-rich, and lime-deficient soils. Plants sensitive to frost should preferably not be placed on such wet soils which, in particular, stay colder in the spring than other soil types since damage caused by a late frost can occur. On the other hand, if your garden has a lime-rich, dry soil with a friable structure and light colour as well, then it will be perfect for plants like thyme (*Thymus*), soapwort (*Saponaria officinalis*), lavender (*Lavandula*), evening primrose (*Eunothera*), and acacia (*Robinia*).

Moving soil

Not everyone will want to adapt their planting completely according to soil type. The choice of plants can, in fact, be broadened by making a few changes to the surroundings. For example, you could build different levels into your garden. By lowering a part of it you can create a pond or a marshland environment. The soil which is thus removed can be used to make an elevation on which plants liking dry soils can grow. If you come up against naturally nutrient-rich soil, but nonetheless want to find a suitable position in the garden for plants

Gravel and stones can be used as ground cover. Warmth absorbed by them during the day lets the soil below stay warm longer. Water can still permeate. However, using stones or gravel will not add any nutrients or humus to the soil.

33

from poorer soils, then you can also introduce variations in ground level. In this case, soil in the higher sections must never be fed. The nutrients initially contained in this raised ground will wash down to the lower sections, creating nutrient-rich and nutrient-poor areas in your garden.

A nutrient-rich, heavy soil can be made poorer by working a large quantity of sand into the upper layer. Poor, lower soil can be brought to the surface by digging the soil over deeply where the upper soil is rich in food and the lower soil deficient.

Soil improvement   The "soil movements" mentioned above are, of course, not appreciated by soil organisms. Furthermore, just try working sand into a clay soil, or digging the ground over. The days when people had an army of staff at their command are gone. Even so, we can improve soil, preferably by natural means, by taking only a little action. Sandy soil can be improved by adding fine clay particles to it. A clay powder, such as bentonite, is used for this. Moreover, the level of organic material must be continually topped up by adding compost and, if necessary, manure. Clay soil should also be fed with compost. Organic material such as peat can be used since this soil is already naturally rich in nutrients. Stronger growth can be encouraged in a weak, peat soil by using powdered basalt or rock.

In the years following your initial activity, these powders can be mixed into the upper soil between your plants. Peat and compost can be put on top of the soil and worked in gently with a rake. All this organic material will have to be replaced regularly.

Compost   You kill many birds with one stone by using compost in your garden. Compost is humus, and it has already been seen how this improves soil structure and hydrology. Soil life feeds on it and compost has value as fertilizer for plants. Regularly fertilizing the soil with compost keeps it "refreshed". An ornamental garden with plants chosen to fit with the soil type should have sufficient fertilizer from compost alone.

While compost can be bought, you may not know exactly what is in it. You can make your own compost heap, of course, in which case you will be able to decide on its composition yourself. In this way you could produce compost with a higher nutrient level by adding droppings to it from rabbits, guinea pigs, chickens, and birds.

Always locate a compost heap in the shadow of trees or bushes to stop it from drying out too quickly. First, loosen up a 1.5m (5ft) width of soil well and cover this with a layer of roughly cut material, necessary for good drainage. Place on top of this a layer 20–25cm (8–10in) thick of roughly cut-up organic waste material from the home, kitchen, or garden. This layer is best laid in one go. Therefore, waste material must be kept separately at first. A very thin layer of lime is then scattered over this as well as a small layer of old compost or garden soil. Yet another layer is placed on top of this, and once again covered over with lime and soil. Continue building it up in this manner until you reach a height of 1.5m (5ft). The heap should then be covered with a layer of straw, or grass clippings, or an old piece of carpeting. Now leave the heap alone for three months. Afterwards, transfer the heap to a place nearby which has been kept free for it. The heap is turned inside-out in the process and decomposition carries on. The compost can be used after another three months.

The addition of lime is necessary to enable quick decomposition. The soil layer is needed to introduce bacteria to the heap. A composter can sometimes be used, particularly for material such as hedge clippings that rots down with difficulty.

Forbidden material on compost heaps Never throw potato peelings which have been sprayed with an anti-sprouting substance onto a compost heap. This substance halts growth, which is the last thing you want from your future compost. Anti-fungal sprays used on citrus fruits are also deadly. These kill off the fungi necessary for breaking down organic material. While weeds which have gone to seed are allowed, I would sooner not run the risk. You cannot be certain that the temperature in the heap will rise high enough to destroy them. Cooked food should never be allowed on the compost heap: this attracts cats, dogs, and rats. Do not throw any

Before putting garden waste on the compost heap, it can be put into a container first.

cabbage stalks with club root on to the compost heap. This rampant fungal disease is impossible to eradicate. Neither should you put thick layers of grass or tree leaves on to the heap. Instead mix these up with lighter material, otherwise no air will be able to pass through. They will then form fixed layers and not decompose.

A well-built compost heap produces excellent garden fertilizer.

Manuring Planting in most ornamental gardens is not always exactly adapted to the precise requirements of the soil. The plants in your garden are continuously using up food while the humus level in the soil is continuously depleting. Large quantities of manure are not always worked into every compost heap, therefore plants should be given both manure and compost every year. In the spring, 400kg (880lbs) of rotted horse manure should be applied per 100m^2 (120sq yds) of border, plus 300kg (660lbs) of compost. Especially demanding plants like roses need approximately half as much again.

In the autumn, cover the border with a layer of mulch 5cm (2in) thick.

Advice for the lawn differs. This is, in fact, a monoculture. A lot of nutrients are lost annually due to all the mowing. Various special lawn fertilizers have been developed. Look out for one which, as well as nutrients, contains micro-organisms for breaking down cellulose. These micro-organisms break down grass mowings left behind and stop them forming a dry crust. For this reason, grass mowings should preferably be left on the lawn after such a treatment. 10kg (22lbs) of fertilizer per 10m^2 (12sq yds) are sprayed on the lawn twice a year, in March and August.

Soil and acidity

The terms "acid soil" and "degree of soil acidity" are very confusing. Acid soils do not naturally contain any lime or chalk. The bacteria needed to convert organic material into food absorbed by plants multiply and work more slowly than in a lime-rich or alkaline soil. As a result, acid soils can contain a lot of non-decomposed vegetation, which – while more moisture-retentive – does not make them any more fertile.

The family of ericaceous plants (heathers) really covets this acid, nutrient-poor soil.

The soil's lime content is measured in pH, also known as the degree of soil acidity. A pH of 7 is neutral, less than this (e.g. 6.5) being acid, while a higher reading (e.g. 7.5) is referred to as being alkaline or basic, and therefore a lime-rich soil.

All soil has its own ideal lime content. The pH for clay soils should be around 7; for sandy soils this may vary between 5 and 6; sandy clay soil should be around 6.5, and for peat soil the ideal pH should be between 5 and 5.5. By adding lime to the soil, the acids already present will be neutralized and nutrients will be released.

Lime in heavy soils binds the fine particles together and makes the structure looser.

TIP

If you want to find out more about your soil's condition, you can always have it investigated professionally.

TIP

Acid rain is caused by gas emissions combining with water vapour. These gases, coming from heavy industry, traffic, and agriculture, come to earth like an acid manure.
At present, the only solution is to lime acid-vulnerable soil.

The garden's green mantle

This chapter looks at the function and effect of trees, conifers, shrubs, and the lawn, "the greenery" in the garden in fact. How were these elements used in the past, and can they be employed in the often smaller gardens of today?

A majestic horse chestnut.

Trees – *always impressive*

Trees have always had an important place in people's lives. You only have to consider the Tree of Knowledge of good and evil in the Garden of Eden. In earlier times, the key-players in large gardens and the countryside were mainly oak (*Quercus*), horse chestnut (*Aesculus*), beech (*Fagus*), birch (*Betula*), yew (*Taxus*), lime or linden (*Tilia*), plane (*Platanus*), and ash (*Fraxinus*).

Law was discussed under the lime trees. The branches were even cut away at different levels so that people could celebrate around and in the tree. Using a ladder, people could climb up to the tree's "second floor".

Trees in the past

As well as lime trees, the fruit tree was a typical feature of the small garden in the Middle Ages. Only later on did these trees make an appearance in the gardens of the rich. In the baroque period, low-growing box and clipped yew trees allowed a panoramic view over the parterres, and long avenues of trees and boscage were established further away from the house, often incorporating topiary. These avenues were sometimes raised and surrounded the various garden sections. Ladies could then saunter round the garden without exposing their skin to the sun and were still able to enjoy all the surrounding beauty.

Not only did the lime tree have the most important position on the village green and in the principal gardens and parks; it held, above all,

38

a permanent position in the farmyard. They were often planted as an espalier in front of the farmhouse, providing cool shade in summer and protection against the rain and wind of autumn and winter. It was also a pleasant bonus that lime trees ensured (and still do) delicious honey.

The tree as an oxygen manufacturer

A tree is a living entity whose leaves take in carbon dioxide from the air aided by sunlight, while its roots absorb water, minerals, and oxygen from the soil. It produces carbohydrates from this which it needs for growth and the formation of leaves and buds. The tree's capacity to do this comes from its chlorophyll. This is what gives leaves their green colour, absorbing sunlight and then transforming and using it to create carbon. Oxygen which humans and animals need to breathe is released during this process.

This greenery is the only oxygen producer on earth and that is the crucial reason for holding it in such high regard. If you are wondering whether to have a certain tree chopped down to make room for some shrubs and perennials, just consider that one old tree produces more oxygen and "captures" more carbon dioxide than hundreds of young new trees. A beech tree a hundred years old with a leaf surface area of 1,500m² (16,000sq ft) – the beech tree itself taking up only 150m² (1,600sq ft) of space – would be able to provide ten people with their annual oxygen intake. Moreover, the foliage of such large trees takes

An espalier of trained lime trees fronting a farmhouse gave protection against sun, wind, and cold.

up an extra 2.83m² (100cu ft) of carbon dioxide and can repeat this after every shower of rain. Therefore, there is every good reason to grow trees in particular.

A tree next to the patio provides shade and security.

The tree in present-day garden design

Trees form the garden's roof and evoke a protected, enclosed feeling which remains even after the leaves have fallen in winter. They enliven a garden, especially in winter, when so many plants have disappeared underground and the garden seems empty, providing a silhouette and also giving protection to birds. Birds will nest in the trees in spring. Trees allow you to enjoy the very best from each new season. You can sit pleasantly in their shade in the spring and summer. A tree which throws some shade on to a patio is welcomed by people who do not want to sit in the sun but who do want to sit next to you (and it saves you from getting an unstable sunshade). Above all do not forget to have a little tree shading the children's play area against the hottest sun of the day. A tree provides much cooler shade than a parasol, the wall of a house, or a lean-to.

A well-placed tree in the garden's foreground adds more depth, making the garden seem larger. A tree offers security, makes a garden more welcoming, and gives people a sense of protection. This is figuratively and literally true, since they hold back the wind, or rather, form a wind-break and maintain air moisture. A tree with a distinctive

Trees with a distinctive growth pattern can – when repeated regularly – strengthen a garden's structure.

shape can strengthen a garden's visual structure when repeated regularly throughout.

Sitting under a small tree, perhaps an apple, in the middle of the herb garden, you could even imagine yourself to be a fair damsel (or daring knight) from the Middle Ages.

A screen of trained lime trees placed not too far from the house still keeps the sun at bay, even nowadays.

Enough food for all the greenery

If you think that the tree's shadow is restricting the growth of other plants, remember that these plants' growth suffers mostly from a lack of nutrients and moisture.

Many plants and shrubs can grow in the shade if given a good amount of compost every now and then. A deep-rooting tree can be encouraged by putting a mixture of leaf mould and mature cattle manure in the soil. This mixture is used to fill in holes made around the tree with a soil drill.

Air for the roots

Just as important as the tree's trunk and crown are the roots which we cannot see. Prepare the ground carefully before you start planting. It is important not to mix up the soil you have dug out. Keep the upper soil on top and do not mix it up with the lower soil! Dig a hole that is at the very least slightly bigger than the diameter of the root ball. Mix the excavated soil with compost (do not forget the different layers),

41

and put a small mound of this mixture in the well-loosened base of the hole you have made. Place the root ball on top of this and fill in the hole bit by bit. Use a blunt stick to press earth well between the roots. If the soil is dry you should now give it a good watering. Keep on filling up the hole with the mixture and press down the soil well. Cover the surface with a layer of compost.

Young trees in windy positions may need a supporting pole on their windward side. It might seem like a lot of work for such a small tree but do not forget that the tree has to be comfortable in this position for years to come.

An exposed area around the tree bole is needed to avoid competition between the grass and tree roots. This also avoids damage to the trunk when mowing.

What you can and cannot do

Remember throughout this operation that tree roots must be able to go on breathing and so need to grow in an aerated soil. This means that a tree cannot be planted in the middle of an asphalted or paved area. Always keep an open space around the tree-trunk within the drip line (tips of the longest branches). Tile paving is another option if this contains sufficient holes.

Do not put down salt on a path which runs past a tree. No plant can withstand this and will react by showing discoloration and withering of the leaves.

When planting new trees, attention should be paid to their location in relation to gas pipes. Leaking gas pipes will suffocate the tree, and tree roots will damage the gas pipes.

TIP

Do not use any manure when planting. The tree only needs to become established in its first year. Manure prevents it from doing anything. If you want to give it something extra use potting compost. You can give the tree manure when it starts growing in its second year.

Trees up to a height of 8m (25ft)

There is nothing more awful than planting a beautiful, young tree only to have to cut it down out of necessity fifteen years later. It never occurred to you that your Indian bean-tree, *Catalpa bignonoides*, would grow such an enormous crown.

People often think that they can limit a tree's size by pruning, but unfortunately this is not the case.

Trees can be grouped into three orders of size, the third order of trees being no taller than 8m (25ft) and thus suitable for smaller gardens. Included amongst these are some less frequently planted kinds which remain small in size.

If you are looking for some attractive trees from the maple family, then *Acer negundo* 'Variegatum' and *Acer griseum* spring to mind. The former has leaves with a beautiful, silvery margin, and a slightly pinkish tint when they first appear. It has a broad, rounded crown and does well in light soils. *Acer griseum* is most attractive with its copper-coloured bark which peels off the trunk and main branches like paper. Its leaves turn a crimson red in autumn. *Acer globosum* is a well-known bushy tree. You should not wait years before pruning as its dense wood is extremely hard. If you like trees with an attractive bark then you should consider the green-white striped bark of *Acer pensylvanicum*. Acers are sun-lovers and will grow in almost all soil types so long as they are not too wet.

The juneberry, *Amelanchier lamarckii* 'Robin Hill', is a kind of

A creeper can grow into a tree within a few years. Take note that creepers can store water and snow in their foliage which can result in branches breaking off due to the increased weight that the tree has to bear.

Trees are irreplaceable as producers of oxygen, especially large, mature trees.

shrubby currant which can be used as a round-shaped tree. It has pink flowers in the spring and requires at least three hours of sunshine every day. It is attractive alongside narrow driveways. Somewhat taller is the golden alder, *Alnus incana* 'Aurea', with its yellow leaves. The trunk and branches are a brownish-yellow, making a splendid combination with its orange-yellow catkins.

Trees create privacy in a garden.

Everything is perfection about the katsura tree, *Cercidiphyllum japonicum*. Its broad, oval crown provides adequate shade for your patio; its reddish-brown twigs produce small, round leaves which emerge pink in colour. During the summer they have a bluish-green underside and the autumn colours are spectacular. Although they do not like clay soils this can be improved whilst planting.

Many attractive kinds of cornel can be grown as trees. The following kinds are of note for their flowers and leaves. *Cornus mas* has yellow flowers in the winter; *Cornus controversa* has laterally growing branches forming layers and produces quite large, white flowers in June. It is suited to all nutrient-rich soils.

The Chinese-lantern tree, *Koelreuteria paniculata*, has a broad, sparsely spread crown. It has pinnate leaves made up of ovate, deeply toothed leaflets which first appear reddish in colour and become yellow in the autumn. In August, showy plumes of yellow flowers are produced which later become bladder-like fruits. It enjoys a nutrient and lime-rich soil.

> **TIP**
>
> It may be necessary to fix a young tree to a supporting pole. Note that this should not be more than 60cm (2ft) above ground level. Otherwise strong winds will cause too much movement of the root ball, preventing it from growing well or quickly.

The medlar, *Mespilus germanica*, is quite well known, but I list it here anyway because of its frequent appearance in gardens from the past. It is in fact a many-branched bush, but with patience and pruning it can be made into a tree. Perhaps an idea for the kitchen garden? *Mespilus germanica* 'Westerveld' is heavy fruiting and hardy against frost. Its soil needs to be moisture retentive.

The Magellan beech, *Nothofagus antarctica*, is a small tree or many-branched bush with a wide, spreading crown. Its herringbone-style growth, pretty bark, and elegant branches create an attractive picture, also in winter. The tiny leaflets turn yellow in the autumn. This is a "translucent" tree suited to semi-shade, and can be placed next to a pond as its leaves are so small. It should not be planted in very heavy soil.

If you are searching for a perfectly round shape buy either a standard or half-standard size *Prunus fruticosa*. This has thin, reddish twigs and branches and very small, dark-green leaves. Its small, white flowers produce red fruits half an inch in diameter. The rounded shape is natural to this slow-growing tree. They look very attractive planted alongside lanes.

The hop-tree, *Ptelea trifoliata*, with its wide, open crown is a half-standard (which can also be grown as a standard). The few shoots branching off the main stem have a pungent scent. The leaf is composed of three lobes which have a leathery feel to them. It has

Prunus fruticosa, *available in various heights, has a naturally rounded shape.*

large bunches of yellow-green, sweet-smelling flowers. Winged fruits appear later in the year which, with a little imagination, do look like bunches of hops. It has the same yellow, autumn colours as the Magellan beech.

The pear, *Pyrus calleryana* 'Chanticleer', has a narrow, conical shape with healthy, shiny-green leaves which turn yellow, orange, and red in autumn. The leaves fall very late (a big problem for tree-growers). Its abundant, white blossom can be enjoyed as early as March. For preference, *Pyrus salicifolia* 'Pendula' should be bought as a standard. The branches hang somewhat downward which explains the word "pendula". It develops a broad crown and has willow-like, grey-felty leaves. Its cream-coloured blossom appears concurrently with its coming into leaf.

The clammy locust tree, *Robinia viscosa*, is a rather less well-known *Robinia* with a broad rounded crown and spreading branches; the young shoots and petioles (leaf-stalks) are dark red and sticky. In contrast to other acacias, this *Robinia* has few thorns. The leaves are long and feathered with many alternate leaflets. In May and June, and for a second time in August, its flowers hang down in large, 8cm (3in) long bunches and are a pale lilac-pink colour.

There are also many short-stature trees to be found amongst the ornamental apples (*Malus*), the ornamental cherries (*Prunus*), the hawthorns (*Crataegus*), and the rowans (*Sorbus*). As well as this,

The shaded privacy of this sitting area is provided by a roof of pruned plane trees.

there are a few trees from the familiar, larger tree genuses which can be pruned successfully and so kept under control or, if you prefer, kept small. For example, the lime tree, *Tilia*, can be trained. The large-leafed lime, *Tilia platyphyllos*, the common lime, *Tilia* x *vulgaris* 'Pallida', and the *Tilia* x *vulgaris* 'Black Lime' are usually used for this very purpose.

The London plane tree, *Platanus acerifolia*, with its peeling bark, can also be trained to grow a roof. Such a "roof" is very useful in formal as well as informal gardens.

The black mulberry, *Morus nigra*, can just be included amongst third-order trees – up to 8m (25ft). This used to be a common sight in gardens. It produces bitter-sweet, almost black, fruits. Unfortunately, these fall off quickly when ripe and will leave marks on any underlying paving.

The white mulberry, *Morus alba*, would not be amiss in your garden either. In fact, it will become a little bigger with a broader crown. The young shoots are prone to frost. Fortunately, both mulberries take well to pruning. A mulberry makes an attractive sun-shade next to a patio, but choose a white mulberry since its fruit will not leave stains behind.

Graceful conifers
Conifers are literally cone-bearers. The yew tree, *Taxus*, belongs to this group too, even though it has waxy berries. Conifers are encountered in all garden styles, old and new. While fancifully shaped pine trees occupied ancient Chinese informal gardens, cypresses (*Cupressus*) fittingly set the dominant overtone in French and Italian formal gardens. Several "new" coniferous trees were brought to Europe in the nineteenth century by botanical hunters. The apogee in gardening of the time was a conifer like the monkey puzzle, *Araucania araucana*, or a Douglas fir (*Pseudotsuga menziesii*), as centrepiece to an ornamental border. And the yew, of course. This has already been mentioned. Beautiful shapes could and can be created with yew, and grateful use has always been made of it. Nowadays, many different conifer genuses and species are used for hedging.

Where do they belong?
The majority of conifer genuses and species have a rigid pyramidal or columnar shape. They therefore stand out strongly against bushes and broad-leaved trees which usually have a more spreading growth pattern. They fit best next to shrubby areas of birches (*Betula*), broom (*Cytisus*), and sea buckthorn (*Hippophae*) which, just like conifers, feel at home in a sandy soil.

The Austrian pine, *Pinus nigra*, and the Scots pine, *Pinus sylvestris*, which have become completely established in sandy areas and grow well in gardens there too, look terrible on clay-soil grassland. Junipers, *Juniperus*, look perfect on heathland or in a heather garden, but look ridiculously out of context in a flat landscape.

A conifer is actually best situated amongst other conifers. A conifer hedge is a good example.

Many cultivars and sub-varieties from the various conifer species are available from garden centres. Try to discipline yourself by not planting too many distinctly different types next to each other, for example ones with yellow foliage next to green columnar and round-bluish sorts. Just one distinctive example amongst neutral neighbours will have a far greater effect.

Planting distance: essential!
An appeal: give conifers space! The reason for this is that the widest part of almost all conifers is at ground level *and* also because many "dwarf" types are often on offer. The Atlas cedar, *Cedrus atlantica* 'Glauca', which has been fashionable for ages, must be planted a good 5m (15ft) from neighbouring plants as it will reach a diameter of between 3.5 and 4m (11–13ft) within ten years or so. Its neighbours, meantime, will also be growing.

From experience, you probably know what happens when several conifers grow next to each other. The needles or scales become brown where they touch other trees, and, still worse, the branches will not usually make any new growth after pruning or the removal of another conifer from the area. However, a stand of conifers planted with future growth in mind is at the mercy of the wind and, moreover, will

Opposite page:
Hydrangea sargentiana *has mauve florets.*

48

look unattractive in the first few years. You are better off planting them close together at first: place a few fast-growing examples, often cheaper, between the slower ones. The fast growers can be removed once the conifers start to touch each other.

This technique also applies to low-lying cultivars such as the Chinese juniper, *Juniperus sinensis* 'Aurea', which can reach a height of about 1.5m (5ft) nonetheless. If planted next to the front door, this little tree will grow so large that within five years you will no longer be able to get past.

Transplanting larger conifers

If you had not reckoned on your conifer growing so fast, it can be transplanted with a little extra preparation – even the larger conifers. Most conifers are evergreen. Their roots take up water for the needles and scales which release water vapour all year round. It is necessary for the roots to suffer as little damage as possible during transplantation so they can go on taking up water immediately.

In the spring, cut the roots at a distance of 40cm (16in) from the trunk to a depth of about 40cm (16in), while simultaneously digging a trench. The roots below the root ball should not be cut yet. Fill the trench with leaf mould (no compost as this contains too much lime). The soil in the trench should not be pressed down too firmly. Sometimes it is necessary to support the conifer at this point. Many new root hairs, needed to absorb water and nutrients, will grow out into the leaf mould from the edge of the existing root ball. The root ball should be carefully dug up in the autumn. The underside of the root ball is then cut away and placed immediately into the new hole. This hole is also filled with leaf mould. Keep the root ball well watered during transplantation. The conifer should be supported again if necessary.

The autumn has been chosen for transplantation because it is traditionally rainy. As a result, the conifer gets plenty of extra watering.

Shrubs, the garden's framework

One can be fairly brief concerning times gone by. Shrubs were grown, of course, in classical times, the Middle Ages, the Renaissance, and during the baroque period. However, it is noticeable that designed gardens had only a limited number of species and that they were also all very severely pruned.

Cotton lavender (*Santolina*), lavender (*Lavandula*), and other small shrubs have been used in particular to make low, trimmed border-hedging around parterres since the Renaissance. Yew, a conifer, produced a higher, trimmed hedge. Just like box, which only started appearing in ornamental gardens in the baroque, yew was used to make all manner of topiary shapes.

Only when more importance was attached to nature, at the end of the eighteenth and beginning of the nineteenth centuries, did many shrubs slowly start to be admitted into gardens without artificiality or

TIP

A tree, whether surrounded by grass or paving, should always have an open space around it within the drip-line.

The space needed to limit competition between the young tree's roots and the grass next to its trunk is 60 x 60cm (24 x 24in) for a trunk circumference of up to 20cm (8in) measured at a height of 1m (3ft) from the ground. This also allows as much moisture and air as possible to enter the soil. This open space may be covered with organic matter.

pruning. They were given such a permanent position, firstly with the introduction of the landscape style and later in borders, that since then it has been impossible to imagine a garden without them.

The introduction of rhododendrons to Europe around 1750 particularly revolutionized gardening. They were placed in "woodland gardens" alongside other hitherto little known shrubs and trees.

The transitionary stage between trees and herbaceous plants

Almost all the characteristics shown by trees are also applicable to shrubs but, because they are usually lower lying, these characteristics are on a smaller scale.

Sometimes it is difficult to judge whether a woody plant is a tree or shrub, but just remember that a tree first produces a stem from which branches shoot, whereas a shrub will have many branches growing at ground level.

Since most shrubs have multiple stems they take up much more room on the ground than does a tree. This is sometimes forgotten when planting. A garden is given its "face" as soon as a few shrubs have been planted in it.

Shrubs are eye-catching to the observer and, in the main, determine the framework of a garden, especially when no trees have been planted.

Rhododendrons are above all shrubs for woodland gardens.

T I P

Trees and shrubs can lengthen your flowering season in a mixed border when combined with annuals, biennials, perennials, bulbs, and tuberous plants. Shrubs in a mixed border provide support and protection for the other plants and ensure that the border is not bare in winter.

Planting distances related

You have planted a nice, little mock orange, *Philadelphus*, which had three branches about 70cm (28in) in length when it was bought. After two years it has to be removed because it has grown 2m (6ft) tall since then and just as wide. To avoid this sort of unpleasant surprise in the future take note of the following planting distances:

Height	*Plant distance*
up to 6m (20ft)	3m (10ft)
3–6m (10–20ft)	1.5–3m (5–10ft)
1–2m (3–6ft)	1.5m (5ft)
0.5–1m (20–3ft)	0.75m (30in)
under 0.5m (20in)	0.5m (20in)

Various flowering times

The shrubs which grow in our gardens today generally have especially colourful displays of flowers. One group which flowers before the leaves emerge includes the Chinese witch hazel (*Hamamelis mollis*) and the cornelian cherry (*Cornus mas*). The largest group flowers in the spring, such as guelder rose (*Viburnum opulus*), the mock orange, *Philadelphus coronarius*, and Jew's mallow (*Kerria japonica*).

There is also a group which flowers in summer, including the butterfly bush (*Buddleia davidii*) and hydrangea (*Hydrangea sargentiana*). Many shrubs can be enjoyed in autumn, having beautiful autumn

Trees and shrubs can create beautiful reflections in a pond

colours and bearing fruit which in some cases can be eaten, like the dwarf quince, *Chaenomeles japonica*.

Evergreen or deciduous

There are both evergreen and deciduous species of shrub. The evergreen ones are particularly popular because they keep the garden "alive" in winter. At least there will be something green to look at. While this is unarguably true, these shrubs tend to be a very dark green colour unchanged by the seasons: rather the same all year round in fact. Leave them out altogether then? No, but try to find a balance between these endless evergreens and their more lively, flowering companions with autumn colours. A row of evergreen bushes with deciduous kinds and perennials planted in between can look a little unnatural in winter. The effect is made less artificial when many evergreen shrubs are planted together in the garden as a group.

A free-standing position

A number of free-standing shrubs are included amongst the deciduous kinds. These are best planted on their own and stand out because of their flowers, growth, shape, or colour. Smooth Japanese maple, *Acer palmatum*, and a smoke-tree variety, *Cotinus coggygria* 'Royal Purple', are examples of such free-standing shrubs. The corkscrew hazel, *Corylus avellana* 'Contorta', deserves a place here as well, perhaps. It is certainly beautiful in winter, but will also be noticed in summer too. It then has large, twisted leaves which look a

Amongst all these evergreen shrubs, this lady will not have to worry about peeping toms at any time of year.

little diseased, and so putting it in such a prominent position is a matter of personal taste.

Smooth sumach, *Rhus glabra*, is a real beauty. Beneath its spreading crown is a perfect place to sit. The roots appearing above ground are a disadvantage, but this is compensated for by its beautiful flowers and gorgeously scarlet autumn colours.

If several free-standing types of shrub are planted between other shrubs it can seem as if they are competing with each other for attention, which creates an extremely restless picture. Use these beauties sparingly if you can, particularly in small gardens. Choose just one, or at most two, and plant them in a location where they be distinctive, perhaps next to a pool or patio, and where they will not come into competition with other plants.

Other options Shrubs make quite excellent wind-breaks. They are used a lot as hedges and, if you have the space for it, a living hedge is preferable to a wall or closed wooden fence over which wind will drop into the garden and start to whirl about. Some shrubs and bushes have a tangled or even thorny branch system, and provide birds with edible fruits. Just consider the quinces from *Chaenomeles japonica* and sloes from the blackthorn, *Prunus spinosa*. Grouped together in a quiet part of the garden, they offer birds food and nesting opportunities.

The border's structure can be made especially charming by putting in shrubs amongst the perennials, never mind that there will also be less to maintain.

In small gardens you are practically living on top of the plants. Remember that some bushes like mock orange and cherry laurel, *Prunus laurocerasus* (not actually a true laurel) have rather large leaves which are not so overbearing at a distance, but which can be close to. It perhaps makes more sense, in a small space, to plant a bush with finer leaves such as *Spiraea* or *Indigofera heterantha*.

Sub-shrubs are mavericks

This *is* difficult. At first sight you might list them under herbaceous perennials (and that is the heading under which most of them are listed in the encyclopedias), but on further inspection they do bear a strong resemblance to shrubs. Some of them have been mentioned already: lavender cotton (*Santolina chamaecyparissus*), old English lavender (*Lavandula angustifolia*), but also thyme (*Thymus vulgaris*), the rock rose (*Helianthemum*), sage (*Salvia officinalis*), hyssop (*Hyssopus officinalis*), winter savory (*Satureja montana*), rue (*Ruta graveolens*), shrubby veronica, varieties of hebe, rosemary (*Rosmarinus officinalis*), heath heather (*Erica*) and ling heather (*Calluna*), alison (*Alyssum montanum*), candytuft (*Iberis sempervirens*), and germander (*Teucrium lucidrys*).

Many of these plants will be known to you as herbs, others as flowering plants. Herbs have been used for centuries, not just in herb gardens but also in ornamental gardens as trimmed edging plants for borders.

TIP

It is actually more important to plant a bush for its outline, leaf shape, and leaf coloration than for its flowers.

You will only have about three weeks to enjoy the flowers, while you will have to look at the leaves for eight months or even more.

Rhus glabra *is a solitary shrub with beautiful flowers and gorgeous autumn colours.*

Grass, the green carpet

Believe it or not, the history of grass cover goes back more than 2,000 years. Pliny the Younger wrote of a field of acanthus, probably not the real *Acanthus* but greenery of one single type, nonetheless. Being closely planted together and having a uniform appearance, it would have looked like what we now call grass – a calm, green surface contrasting with the colourful, taller garden plants. It was probably an alternative to the water gardens in the south where Middle-Eastern influences were at their strongest. The Romans tried to create a smooth, green surface too, using all kinds of plants. This was not an easy matter, of course, since the plants had to contend with regular cuttings and mowings (with a scythe). A probable favourite at that time was common camomile, *Chamaemelum nobilis* 'Trenaegue'. Common camomile has continued to be used down the ages as a substitute for the grass lawn. This "grass" was even used to make the medieval turf seats.

Reference is made as early as the twelfth century to fields composed only of grass. These early grass fields did look different from the ones we know today. They were like alpine meadows: the grass was fairly long, containing many flowers and herbs. There was a predilection for daisies (*Bellis perennis*), violets (*Viola*), periwinkle (*Vinca minor*), and primroses (*Primula veris*). In the fourteenth century, turfs were cut from surrounding fields and were laid next to each other in gardens to make a more or less smooth, flat surface. Only much later,

The garden's layout is determined by the paths made from brick and grass.

TIP

The majority of sub-shrubs feel most at home in a Mediterranean environment. In colder climates they should always be pruned back just after the winter, leaving some green shoots visible below the cutting point.

in the nineteenth century, did people start selecting grass types, and the invention of the lawn-mower signalled an explosion in grass lawns. Maintenance was made much easier. A lawn could be mowed more often and more quickly. Herbaceous plants which could not tolerate this weekly "pruning" disappeared of their own accord. True grass cover became a reality.

These straight green, grassy paths unify the different flower borders.

Still the same goal

Grass still fulfils its role as the garden's green carpet. This expanse of green is restful on the eyes; a visible ground level on which you can stand with your own two feet. It is the neutral background against which the various other parts of the garden can stand out well, while also being able to bring a unity to these garden divisions too.

The lawn's big advantage is that it can be walked upon, and not many alternatives to this exist. A patch of grass is indispensable in a garden where children will be playing.

The biggest problem is that so much is expected from a lawn. The single most important factor in laying out a garden is really the neutralizing effect of this green surface.

Grass is double the work

It is sometimes said: "If you don't want a lot of work on your hands in the garden, just have a large lawn." Nothing is further from the truth, in fact. A lawn requires a lot of time, energy, feeding, tools, and an invincible attitude to keep it looking good. And what is your idea of a lawn? An attractive billiard table of fine grass which needs mowing twice weekly? In that case you are better off not having children play on it, and you should rarely walk over it yourself.

A little less problematic is using a mixture of different kinds of grass seed, such as those brought into production for sports pitches and playing fields.

Not as green, but just as attractive

Recently people have been looking back to the past. Just how did flower meadows look? A flower meadow is a piece of land onto which a mixture of seeds from annuals, biennials, or perennials is sown. Bulbous and tuberous plants can also be included amongst these. While such a meadow is a charming sight, it cannot be walked over, neither does it form a neutral or even level "carpet".

Another option is to sow seeds of wild biennials and perennials mixed in with seeds from slow-growing grasses, such as *Agrostis stolonifera*. It may be less colourful, but does come closer to the previously laid down goal for a neutral, green expanse of grass. Paths can be made through this meadow in order to enable you to walk over. Real grass paths will emerge through regular mowing since flowers will then be unable to get a hold.

A flower-covered lawn can also be "self-grown" by letting it deteriorate. Give it absolutely no fertilizer, and rake away all the mown grass (which also contains nutrients). Clover (*Trifolium*),

TIP

Nowadays, special lawn fertilizer products can be bought. Some contain azobacteria which take nitrogen from the air. Furthermore, cellulose-eating fungi may be included which feed on mown grass. Rotting clumps of grass cuttings are now a thing of the past. Lawn-aerator machines can be thrown away.

Grass forms a neutral basis in a garden.

Alternatives to a grass lawn are blanket-growing ground cover plants and mosses.

chickweed (*Cerastium*), yarrow (*Achillea*), and speedwell (*Veronica*) will spontaneously spring up on the bare patches which start to appear. Seeds gathered from the verges in your immediate vicinity can also be sown on these patches of ground.

If it is all taking too long for you and you are uncertain about sowing, then buy some ready-to-plant wild flowers and plant them in the grass. Another option for making a lawn comes from the group of evergreen ground cover plants.

This is something to be considered if your stretch of grass has reached the total renewal stage.

A species of juniper, *Juniperus horizontalis*, pearlwort (*Sagina subulata*), *Cotula squalida*, and *Cotula potentillina* take happily to being walked over.

They do not, in fact, have to be mown, but it will regularly take a good quarter of an hour to pull up the weeds which continuously come up between these plants.

This country garden has been kept restrained. Large numbers of vigorously flowering plants are unnecessary because of all the blue tints.

An artist's palette

If the garden has been laid out and its green framework is in place, it is then time to fill in the lines with colour which can be found in flowers such as roses, perennials, herbaceous plants, annuals, and biennials.

Use of colour

Colour has an important role to play in today's garden. In general, more flowering plants are being used in gardens now than in the past. If you look back through history, it becomes clear that gardens in the Renaissance and baroque, for example, were above all compositions of form and space. Since most people no longer have such an abundance of room with which to indulge themselves in endless avenues, lakes, grottoes, and statuary, attention seems to have been concentrated on colour. Remember that in the very best scenario a plant will flower for a maximum of three months, leaving you to look at its leaves and shape for the rest of the year.

When drawing up a colour scheme for your garden do not forget that colours vary according to light intensity and the angle of the sun. For example, the cool colour blue can be very distinctive in the full midday sun, but the same blue flowers will no longer be visible at twilight, while white flowers do show up well at that time of day. Pastels produce good colour in a damp atmosphere with indirect sunshine, but are bleached out in direct sunlight. In the same way that red and yellow tones are warm colours, blue and white tones are cool. Warm colours seem to approach you whereas cooler colours appear further away. Greys and grey-greens are neutral colours which can bind other ones together. No one should be surprised to learn that green comes across as a calming colour. Yet the colour green has many variations. Just consider a grey-green, bluish-green, and yellow-

Sunlight on a part of the flower-bed has an unexpected effect on colour combination.

green in several gradations. Yellow-green and light green lighten up a shady spot, whereas dark green will create a black hole in the same location.

Often you find by yourself the combination that you are looking for in your garden. Do not be influenced by others. It is all a matter of taste. Moreover, everyone has their own colour range, which means an individual interpretation of colour combinations. Just do what you think looks attractive.

A colour chart can be of assistance in putting colours together. Colours which are opposites to each other provide the maximum contrast while those closely related create harmony.

Remember that colours in a garden are always seen in combination with one another and never separately, and that green is the dominant force in the colour scheme.

The statue's light grey colour balances out the rest.

The rose, queen of all time   Roses deserve a special entry: not under shrubs, even though botanically speaking that is where they belong, but under the perennials – the flowers. Close your eyes to think about roses and you will be imagining clouds of scent and colour.

Rose history goes back millions of years. Their fossils have been found from 30 million years ago. The rose probably originated in Asia. It is known with certainty that the Emperor Nero had discovered its scent and colour because he had streets, temples, and palaces strewn with

Whoever said that green was just green?

rose petals on festive occasions. Unfortunately, he had a problem. Roses in classical times only had a brief flowering season. The Romans found a solution to that. Outside this short season, roses in bud were imported from Egypt.

In the Middle Ages, the rose was associated with the Virgin Mary. The rose could be found depicted in wood and stone carvings, and in glass (rose windows), in churches and monasteries, and in living form, of course, in castle and monastery gardens. There was still not a lot to choose from. *Alba*, *gallica*, *canina*, and *damascena* roses would certainly have been grown. It was not only scent which was important. Rose-hips and rose petals were also used for culinary and medicinal purposes. New discoveries in the Middle Ages included the musk rose *Rosa moschata*, with its musk-smelling leaves and clusters of flowers, and the cabbage rose *Rosa centifolia*. Endless numbers of hybrids were produced.

Developing trade with China in the second half of the sixteenth century brought with it the importation of Chinese roses. These flowered longer and had a richer range of colour, but were not so hardy.

White peps up a garden while too much white has an overdosing effect.

The tea rose

The first hybrid between an eastern and western rose took place by chance on the French island of Bourbon. A hedge of Chinese roses, *Rosa chinensis*, stood next to a hedge of damask roses, *Rosa*

64

damascena. A hybrid arose from this situation, the first long-flowering, hardy rose: the Bourbon rose. A second famous hybrid was from the Chinese rose and a musk rose flowering in South Carolina. This was put on the market in 1819 by the Parisian rose-grower Louis Noisette. The Noisette rose was a richly flowering, strong-smelling rose, but unfortunately not hardy.

Once again, there came another hybrid: this time Chinese roses with Bourbon roses, and later on with Noisette roses. These were the tea roses which had the scent of Chinese tea. Sadly, these hybrids were not hardy. Crosses were made once more: Bourbon roses with French roses. The result was hardy, but with a shorter flowering season. New crosses resulted in the remontant rose which flowered twice a year and carried scented, heavy flowers. In conclusion, the tea rose hybrids had arrived.

At the end of the nineteenth century, the growers Pernet-Ducher provided a sensation: by making crosses with the yellow rose, *Rosa lutea*, from central Asia, the colour yellow was introduced into the tea hybrids, and so the modern yellow rose was born.

The first rose garden   Roses were scattered about gardens up to 1800. This made sense since until then roses only flowered for three weeks at a stretch. The first person to bring in sweeping design changes in this area was Joséphine de Beauharnais. Napoléon made her a gift of the château de

The brilliance of white is suitable for the darker areas of the garden.

Malmaison near Paris, where she had beautiful gardens made. They included an English garden with streams, waterfalls, and little temples, plus a true rose garden: a garden with winding paths and large rose-borders. There were roses against the walls, roses in stands, roses over arches, against lattice-work screens, against pillars and obelisks.

Later in the nineteenth century, when a number of long-flowering rose varieties became available, many flower-beds became filled with roses, having previously been exclusively planted with annuals.

There were some old-fashioned, static garden features which it was found difficult to abandon – for example, a flowering crown of roses, rising up in height. About the crown stood four standard roses like sentries. The crown could be approached from four points. These paths brought you to a path which ended up circling round the whole crown. These days such a rose display would be thought excessive. However, even individual rose-borders contribute to a park look and require a lot of maintenance.

Perseverance and maintenance

It should not be forgotten that roses require a lot of care, even though modern varieties have had many good qualities bred into them. They like a nutrient-rich, well-drained, moist soil which is not too alkaline. Diseases are almost impossible to eradicate and, depending on the problem, expert pruning will have to be done. Some roses will

The Sedum's *flower colour enhances the red of the bricks.*

continue to produce flowers once the dead-heads have been snipped off. Regular manuring should not be forgotten; after all, roses need a great deal of energy to create buds and flowers. The ground underneath roses should be kept weed-free.

And do not forget that all this work takes place in a thorny environment.

Every year, I am tempted to get rid of the *Rosa* 'Mozart' which I once planted to enliven a rather colourless border. It is virtually impossible to work with: to make my way through the border's terrible thorns, I have to be swathed from head to toe in old clothes and, of course, a pair of sturdy, protective gloves.

The off-white rose 'Nevada' flowers copiously in June and July and even some time after that. It is just tall and wide enough to sit beneath comfortably.

Border combinations

Roses are often combined with perennial plants in borders today. In this way it is possible to distract the eye from the rigid shape of most rose-bushes. It is best to choose perennials which do not use up too much of the soil's nutrients, and which are shallow-rooting. Low-growing varieties of yarrow (*Achillea*), rock roses (*Helianthemum hybridum*), succulents (*Sedum*), a number of varieties of thyme (*Thymus*), and veronicas such as *Veronica incana* and *Veronica rupestris* are amongst the plants appropriate for this.

Other combinations can also be considered for camouflaging the exposed underside of rose-bushes, including soaproot (*Gypsophila*), lavender (*Lavandula*), cotton lavender (*Santolina*), peonies

67

(*Paeonia*), and delphiniums (*Delphinium*). These last combinations will be a nuisance to the roses within a few years because of their neighbours' demanding roots which also need food. These perennials will have to be removed after two to three years, the soil needing to be turned over and manured before any subsequent planting. It is better to plant your rose towards the back of the border so that its ugly underside can be easily camouflaged. This entails choosing a taller-growing variety which will show up above the perennials in the foreground.

Why should a rose flower all summer long? There is more than enough choice from colourful perennials and annuals. Their flowers can take over the rose's responsibility, as it were.

Roses, perennials, and shrubs can all be grown together without problems.

I would just like to make a case for roses with particularly attractive leaves. This is, after all, what one has to look at for the other eight months of the year.

Rosa glauca (syn. *Rosa rubrifolia*) has beautiful purple-grey leaves which combine well with various perennials such as *Acanthus* and the masterwort (*Astrantia major*).

The tall and glowingly healthy *Rosa moyesii* 'Geranium' takes up a lot of room and produces really blood red flowers, but for only two or three weeks. However, its rose-hips turn orange from August, lasting way into November.

The colour blue changes depending on the light. This is clearly visible in the foreground.

The spirit of romance

The time of one rose to every stem is somewhat over. People are also moving away from the rigid rose-border and, for preference, want flowers all summer. The modern David Austin rose attempts to unite the scent, colour, and shape of the old roses with the long-flowering and disease-resistant qualities of modern kinds. The 'Heritage' rose is one example: gorgeously soft-pink, plump, and scented flowers. This type is a little on the formal side and the bush grows taller than most catalogues indicate. This is quite a common complaint.

Before buying roses, it is best to go first to a nursery or rose garden to see how they look in practice.

Catalogue illustrations are always stunning but only capture one moment. Will the old flower petals really drop off, or will they hang on, covering the bush in brown clusters? Will the rose's pink colour stay constant whilst in flower, or will it change into a white or mauve? Will the stems become top-heavy with flowers, making the stems bend over so that it will no longer be possible to look into the centre of the flowers?

Shrub roses are also seen planted everywhere. They have a rather more free and natural growth pattern and are exceedingly well suited to being grown in combination with perennials. Simple pastel tones are the principal hallmarks of this group, which includes the very widely known 'Ballerina'. The scarce yellow varieties should also be

English roses have an old-fashioned air, combined with modern characteristics such as disease resistance and long flowering times. This is 'Abraham Darby'.

TIP

Ground-cover roses usually grow no higher than 60cm (24in) and seemingly cover the ground preventing weeds from getting a hold. This is not borne out in practice. And if there are lots of nasty, little spines, as with 'Snowballet', then weeding will become a painful experience. An extra-thick layer of mulch will keep the weeds at bay.

mentioned. 'Golden Wings' is a marvellous lemon-yellow – a tall rose, at least 1.5m (5ft) in height, with single, slightly larger flowers. Its scent is delightful. A large specimen like this is best placed at the back of a border. The stems fanning out from 'Sally Holmes' bear heavy clusters of large, yellow-white, single flowers. As a result, the flowers appear very full. 'Pearl Drift' is the shrub-rose sister to the climber 'New Dawn'.

Cluster roses are also excellent in borders. 'Schneewittchen' combined with lavender or box is widely repeated nowadays. One of the many other kinds of cluster rose is 'Bonica' with full trusses of flowers. This is a very sturdy rose, 90cm (36in) high, vigorous, and with shoots stemming from its base upwards.

Ground cover roses forming large mats or placed in the border foreground are also included amongst the possible options. The repeat-flowering 'Snowballet' has full, white flowers and is attractive alongside the purplish-brown leaves of *Heuchera micrantha* 'Palace Purple'. Snowballet's leaves are a shiny green and are shed late. This rose can be used as a low, spreading hedge.

Rosa 'The Fairy' creates a fairy story of its own in many gardens, with its bright red, full flowers hanging in great trusses. It is very highly recommended in pots as well.

The Damask rose 'Henri Martin' forms a bush 2m (6ft) tall and thrives along a north-facing wall too. Ideal for low walls.

Roses to the sky   The choice of climbing roses, or climbers, is enormous. They do not climb by themselves but have to be fastened. Even the smallest climber will always reach a height of 2.5m (8ft). Therefore, most garden walls and fences are in fact too low. The stems carrying flowers have to be tied up horizontally for support. Does the rose actually like being up against a wall? Absolutely not, unless a great many conditions have been met first. Ensure that there is enough aerated, nutrient-rich soil around its roots. Sand and rubble coming up from the foundations can be a nuisance. Place the rose about 50cm (20in) from the wall. This keeps the roots from becoming instantly overheated, which they do not like. The rose is best fastened to the wall with a gap of about 5cm (2in). This helps air circulate around the stems and leaves. Create enough space for watering as all that foliage results in a lot of evaporation.

Planting a rose against a north-facing wall is not always such a bad idea. Several roses are very comfortable in that position, including the very well-known, light pink *Rosa* 'New Dawn' which, in fact, is not as repeat-flowering as is always stated. At the height of summer it needs at least four weeks to recover before it can start flowering again. The familiar repeat-flowering, yellow rose 'Golden Showers' is also suitable for a north-facing wall with similarly half-full flowers. It has very healthy leaves and fewer thorns.

Roses do not like being planted too close to a wall; they dislike full sunshine and too much warmth on and around their roots.

Rosa 'Mermaid' is a gorgeous, vigorous rose which, unfortunately, is a little sensitive to frost.

More space becomes available when large arches, arcades, and bowers are used: taller roses can be grown over these, such as *Rosa* 'Mermaid'. After a slow start, it will eventually grow much taller than 'Golden Showers'. The 'Mermaid' has lemon-yellow flowers with golden-brown stamens and smells wonderful. Put it in a protected place, in semi-shade or direct sunlight, as it is sensitive to hard frosts.

Rosa 'Schnee-wittchen', often used at the moment.

In many gardens today, rose-bushes are being used as gateways. Very often these roses are used in combination with *Clematis* for a succession of flowers throughout the season or else for the simultaneous combination of splendidly beautiful flowers.

Working with such strong, thorny, woody stems is no easy job. For such combinations, it is probably better to grow the least time-consuming varieties of *Clematis* which flower in summer. These produce flowers from all new shoots and can be cut back to 0.5m (20in) above the ground each spring.

TIP

Only put up rose bowers which are high and wide enough. Remember that roses can also grow outwards, not always following the bower's straight lines.

Ramblers for trees

Ramblers are especially wild and fast-growing roses which are rich in flowers, but only for a short time. A height anywhere from 5 to 7m (16–23ft) is normal. These very natural-looking roses get relegated to the charming little summer-house or the ugly shed which has to be disguised. This is where many such roses have ended up, like *Rosa* 'Mme Alfred Carrière' which is variously listed in the catalogues

under repeat-flowering climbers or else under ramblers. This one enlarges considerably, and a pergola of normal size is soon swamped completely under its luxuriance.

Ramblers seem to like trees as well. It is a little troublesome fastening them to the tree-trunk; how should you really go about it? Is it better to wind the long stems around the tree like a kind of spiral staircase, or simply position them straight upwards until they reach the first branches?

Make no mistake, they will grow rampantly in a tree. This will not cause you real problems, but you will want to remove dead wood (which can prick you just as badly as when alive). Real pruning, or now and then removing an old stem, will not be successful. The whole rose becomes entwined with the tree. However, it will look beautiful, especially in old fruit trees which no longer produce their former yield but which have a pleasantly gnarled shape and attractive bark.

The pear tree first flowers with fabulous, white blossom and a good month later it flowers again, or that is what you will think at first sight. In fact, it is the scented *Rosa* 'Seagull' with its clusters of white flowers and yellow stamens.

There are also 'Bobby James', 'Wedding Day', and the species rose *Rosa longicuspis*. There are many more besides, all flowering briefly but heavily with cream or white flowers and a slightly yellow centre, all equal in size, and all very similar in appearance.

The summer-flowering rose and clematis can be pruned back simultaneously in the spring.

Perennials Even 2,000 years before Christ, the Persians were using flowers such as anemones, sweet William, carnations, lilies, and violets in their gardens. Bulbous plants like tulips and hyacinths were also popular in Persia. A few flowering bushes including roses, lilac, and jasmine provided the necessary colour and scent. The climber, honeysuckle, should not be forgotten either.

Rows of flowering plants were also seen in medieval ornamental gardens. The favourites of the time were lily-of-the-valley, periwinkles, peonies, hollyhocks, cowslips, wallflowers, daisies, borage, irises, lilies, pinks, foxgloves, marigolds, violets, columbines, lavender, and mallows.

In the Renaissance, flowers from the east – the tulip, hyacinth, grape hyacinth, and fritillary – as well as flowers from the West such as African marigolds were added to the existing medieval arsenal. Flowers in Renaissance gardens were mostly placed inside beds which were square (done in a chequer-board pattern), rectangular, triangular, or circular. A favourite motif was a star or heart-shaped bed. The flower-beds were symmetrically opposed to one another and separated by small paths. Each of the beds was edged in brick, or with herbaceous plants (not box since its smell was unpopular), and filled with various flowering plants. Flowers in square beds were sometimes planted en masse in just one colour, and sometimes as a mixture of two or three colours (preferably red and white, or yellow and blue).

A border seen from the main room of a house is better appreciated along its length than when seen square on.

TIP

Rambling roses like aerated, nutrient-rich soil too. In borders, ramblers can be planted at a distance of 1m (3ft) from the tree. Where there is grass or paving around the tree, close planting is unavoidable. Plant the rose below ground level in a large container with lots of holes.

Plants were placed in tidy rows, however. Flowers were also planted to form the shape of a coat of arms or an emblem. They were to be found as well in pots and vases wherever paths between beds crossed.

A Renaissance design given contemporary content.

The flower-beds of the Renaissance changed into the *parterres de broderie* of the baroque, made up of box-hedging in arabesque patterns. Towards the end of the seventeenth century, this embroidered style had developed into more abstract patterns which were, nevertheless, always derived from natural subjects such as palm leaves, vine tendrils, or pinks. The open spaces between the box-hedging were "coloured in" with stone chippings, iron filings, coal, and sand.

While such parterres were at first enclosed by a box border, this soon became replaced by the *plate bande*, a flower border.
The Renaissance *pièces coupées pour des fleurs* (chequer-board flower-beds) remained in existence alongside the *parterres de broderie* of the seventeenth century. A new addition was the *parterre à l'anglaise*, a large, separate, grass-filled lawn edged in sand.
The Dutch-style, seventeenth-century *plate bande* surrounding the parterres was never planted to overflowing with flowers. Instead, flowers were planted so that each one had plenty of space to itself and could be appreciated individually.

Many new, flowering plants were imported into Europe from the eighteenth century onwards, including great numbers of perennials. Their form and colour were thought spectacular, but just how they were to be incorporated into what were still mostly formal gardens often caused difficulties. Complex parterres were simplified in many places at that time: a grass parterre surrounded by a flower-border became fashionable. Round flower-beds where new acquisitions could be planted were placed in these grass parterres as well. However, the appeal of geometrical designs continued too. A box broderie was sometimes laid out on the grass with the entire area once again being surrounded by a flower-border. A new development at this time was the use of flowering hanging plants in urns and vases.

In the nineteenth century, new theories were developed concerning colour combinations. Arguments on whether flowers should be planted in combinations or en masse, and whether these should display contrasting colours or gradations of colour, were the order of the day.

It was felt that perennials did not really belong in a flower-planted parterre. Annuals and biennials were primarily responsible for this colourful effect.

New forms of ornamentation using flowers were dreamt up, such as geranium (*Pelargonium*) pyramids and flower carpets. Use of annuals, succulents, and low-growing perennials reached its zenith in

Box was the only living material to give colour to parterres in the original embroidery style – colour was otherwise supplied by stone chippings, iron filings, and coal.

these nineteenth-century flower-borders, where they were planted in minute detail to form geometrical shapes in carpet beds.

A modern farmhouse garden.

Another development was the use of large-leafed foliage plants in formal borders as an alternative to flowers. Examples of plants used for this purpose are Indian shot (*Canna*), the castor oil plant (*Ricinus*), *Coleus*, *Caladium*, *Dieffenbachia*, rhubarb, maize, and cabbage.

Colour, up to the second half of the nineteenth century, can be said to have been employed in rather stiff, formal designs. A reaction against this formality came from England in the second half of the nineteenth century, when William Robinson argued in favour of a more free and natural use of plants.

The border Gertrude Jekyll was originally a painter and approached gardens more from the plants' point of view. From 1890 she involved herself in garden design in which combinations of perennials in long, wide borders had a high profile. These borders were far wider than the beds surrounding grass parterres. Furthermore, they could be irregular shapes and were by no means always placed alongside a lawn.

Gertrude Jekyll sang the praises of the cottage garden, a sort of farmhouse garden whose date of origin is uncertain. Luxuriantly flowering, decorative plants were also to be found in the often

TIP

The following plants are suitable for carpet bedding: pearlwort (*Sagina*), wall-cress (*Arabis*), *Echeveria*, and the succulents *Sempervivum* and *Sedum* with many varieties of leaf colour.

separate areas of orchard, fruit garden, and kitchen garden. The owners of these gardens had probably been employed since times long past as gardeners on the outlying estates. It is quite likely that now and then a cutting or some seeds were taken home, since buying ornamental plants would have been beyond their means! There was not much time to look for the right position, never mind following a planned layout. Such plants were often placed alongside the garden path up to the front door, or in a row under the windows. Plants had to grow wherever chance had set them down. This explains the cottage garden's happy-go-lucky exuberance.

Waves of colour   The first perennial borders were rectangular in design and content, but Gertrude Jekyll dared to group plants (irregularly) of differing heights and shapes next to, or behind, one another. She felt that colours should gently meld into each other to create the impression of a painting. Foliage plants, with their various tones of green, also found a place in her borders. The plants which grew best in cottage gardens were her favourites too. The course of time had proved their hardiness.

Characteristic, cottage-garden plants will certainly feature should you want to re-create a Jekyll-style border. Bluebell bulbs (*Hyacinthoides non-scriptus*) and *Scilla* must be given a place, as well as peonies

A jumble of colours in a cottage garden.

(*Paeonia officinalis*), catmint (*Nepeta* x *faassenii*), the double-flowered soapwort (*Saponaria officinalis* 'Rosa Plena'), arabis (*Arabis caucasica*), woundwort (*Stachys byzantina*), anchusa (*Anchusa azurea*), the yellow-leafed tansy (*Tanacetum parthenium* 'Aureum'), euphorbias (*Euphorbia chariacas* ssp. *Wulfenii*), saxifrage (*Bergenia cordifolia*), sneezewort (*Achillea ptarmica* 'The Pearl'), irises including *Iris sibirica* and *I. pallida*, lilies (*Lilium candidum* and *L. regale*), evening primrose (*Oenothera missouriensis*), foxgloves (*Digitalis purpurea*), the castor oil plant (*Ricinus communis*), Indian shot (*Canna indica*), plantain lilies (*Hosta sieboldiana* and *H. plantaginea*), cranesbills including (*Geranium himalayense* and *G.* x *magnificum*), Carpathian bellflowers (*Campanula carpatica*), mullein (*Verbascum phlomoides*), lupins *(Lupinus)*, oriental poppies (*Papaver orientalis*), maiden pinks (*Dianthus caryophyllus*), yarrow (*Achillea filipendulina*), valerian (*Centranthus ruber*), hollyhocks (*Althaea rosea*), delphiniums (*Delphinium*), *Acanthus*, forget-me-nots (*Bellis perennis*), iris (*Iris*), lady's mantle (*Alchemilla mollis*), lavender (*Lavandula*), Geraniums, day lilies (*Hemerocallis* 'Flore Pleno'), *Clematis* in several varieties including herbaceous kinds, and roses. Used in addition to this are many spring and summer-flowering bulbous and tuberous plants, as well as many annuals and biennials. For example, Gertrude Jekyll used Indian cress (*Tropaeolum majus*)

Emphasis has been placed only on the flowers in this cottage garden. Colour harmony is of less importance here.

Only in the Netherlands are plate bandes seen where flowers are planted separated from one another.

79

to grow over plants whose flowering season had finished, such as soaproot (*Gypsophila paniculata*). She repeated the same trick with sweet peas (*Lathyrus grandiflorus*), which distracted attention away from the dead heads of early-flowering perennials, and provided a replacement for these vacant spaces. It is often said that Gertrude Jekyll worked a great deal in pastels. From the above list it can be seen that this is completely untrue.

Do not over-concentrate on the pretty flowers and flowering times of perennials and annuals. Many perennials, biennials, annuals, and bulbous plants have wonderful leaves too, like the many varieties of saxifrage, giant cow parsnip (*Heracleum mantegazzianum*), several varieties of *Rodgersia*, common butterbur (*Petasites hybridus*), *Kirengeshoma palmata*, Christmas roses (*Helleborus* varieties), New Zealand burr (*Acaena* varieties), barrenwort (*Epimedium*), plantain lilies (*Hosta* varieties), the toad lilies (*Tricyrtis*), *Veratrum* varieties, and *Euphorbia* varieties.

The ideal concept A border is most attractive seen from an angle. Plants not in flower and any gaps there may be will not then be noticed. Jekyll pointed this out as well. Borders in her time were yards long: there was more than enough space. Width had to be a minimum of 2.4m (8ft) if plant variety and flowering were to be guaranteed from late spring until late

The purple columbine and the white foxglove are typical cottage-garden plants.

autumn. Since then, we have come to the present-day conclusion that some of this width can in fact be cut back, but a width approaching 2m (6ft) is still needed to create a vigorous ensemble of colour, flower types, and leaf shapes.

In the first borders, a ramp of plants had to be built up where tall ones were placed at the back with shorter ones at the front. Gertrude Jekyll went against this rule too.
She allowed a few tall plants to grow up between the lower ones for a more natural effect.

And then the soil. This was absolutely not allowed to be seen. Every inch of soil was occupied. If any plants should leave gaps in the course of the year then these were filled in an instant by pot plants and border plants.

Graham Thomas, who can still remember Gertrude Jekyll's garden, recalls: "When you saw those beautiful borders with all their gradual changes in colour, it was just like walking through a rainbow."

Shelter and support   Many traditional gardens were once enclosed by walls and hedges against trespassers, but considered most popular as backdrop to a border was a hedge of dark-green yew, *Taxus baccata*, against which

TIP

An island flower-bed might interest you if you have a lot of space and large lawns. This was used as early as the 19th century as a variation on the rectangular parterres. Place either a circle or an oval in the grass. This border can be appreciated from many points of view. As a rule, such borders have some wind-related problems.

A border alongside a garden path is usually a success because it is viewed lengthways and not face on.

perennials' colours showed up well. A sizeable area was always left unplanted between hedge and border. Such areas can still be found today. Tasks such as weeding and tying up plants at the back of the border then become easy to perform. The hedge could also be clipped and its roots cut back.

Borders situated up against hedges contain poor-growing plants at the back. The hedge's roots take a lot of food and water away from them.

All gardeners can depend on Rosa 'New Dawn' – *this rose will grow everywhere.*

TIP

Once in every three or four years perennials need to be separated. Split the plant up into several pieces. Ensure that each new piece has three to five buds or new shoots (and enough roots). The centre of the original plant is old: it contains little new life. Throw this middle section away.

Where there was little space, fences or trellice-work partitions were also employed. When grown over by creepers, such constructions perform like hedges by filtering out the wind. A wall was also used in the past as a background. This had the added advantage of absorbing heat and thus offering a location for the more warmth-loving plants. A wall completely blocks wind. Drop-winds and whirlwinds can arise because of this.

Perennials could not be allowed to fall over, of course, or the whole effect would be lost. Much attention was given to securing them. Many methods from the past are still employed today. The stems of very tall plants, such as delphiniums for example, were tied to bamboo sticks placed behind them. For the medium-sized plants, several sticks were put in place to which the plants were attached as a group by raffia or string.

Bushy plants like *Nepeta sibirica*, *Artemisia lucoviciana*, soaproot

(*Gypsophila* varieties), anchusa (*Anchusa azurea*), and speedwell varieties such as the taller *Veronica longifolia* and *V. spicata* were held upright nicely by planting twigs – from the hazel, *Corylus avellana*, for example – around and amongst the groups of plants.

Usually there was enough gardening staff to accomplish this work. As always, the problem is to do it enough in advance. This chore should be started at the beginning of May, depending somewhat on the spring in question.

Fortunately, several practical means of supporting plants can now be purchased, even if they are not all as attractive. A skilful person might be able to produce something attractive themselves from old waste material.

A particularly functional way to provide support.

The mixed border

Even though the perennial border is still highly praised by many, it should be honestly admitted that many of us can no longer provide the labour such borders entail. Most of us do not have an army of gardeners at our beck and call to manure the plants (every plant having its own requirements), or regularly to restock, weed, secure, dig, and re-style our borders. It is certainly true that borders are beautiful from the end of spring until mid-autumn, but for the rest of the time there is little to experience.

The mixed border provides a solution. It has perennials, annuals, biennials, and herbaceous plants amongst, and in front of, the shrubs and trees, and there is also room for tuberous and bulbous plants. The mixed border is less work intensive: less needs to be supported and tied up. Shrubs provide support in the mixed border, and also serve as a wind-break. It is also better when choosing the ideal spot for all the flowering plants. The flowering times for this border are longer and there is still something to see in winter.

TIP
Try letting a bush which only flowers in spring be the support for a herbaceous, summer-flowering Clematis. How about a blue-flowered *Clematis* x *durandii* growing over your evergreen rhododendron?

Herbaceous plants

Herbaceous plants have a separate place in our artist's palette. I am placing them in this chapter since they are mostly planted in gardens nowadays because of their flowers.

Many "flowering plants" could be seen growing in medieval gardens which were specifically designated as "herb gardens", even going back about ten centuries.

Healing herbs

People have grown herbs with the intention of becoming better from them for as long as there have been gardens. Hippocrates, the father of western medicine, registered 400 useful, herbaceous varieties. In the first century B.C., the Greek doctor Dioscorides wrote his great work *De Materia Medica*. Six hundred herbs were included in this with meticulous descriptions of their curative powers. This work is still cited even today.

In the Middle Ages, healing herbs were chiefly grown in monastery gardens. The monastery's inner court was used originally as an

A mixed border is attractive all year round.

ornamental garden, comprising grass with flowers. The central garden was crossed by two paths. Around this courtyard ran a cloister. Monks, having a knowledge of Greek and Latin, translated books containing information on herbs, which thus enabled the friars and fathers to serve the community.

In the sixteenth century, the ornamental lawns in these courtyards were gradually dug up and replaced by herbs.

Within castles' defences there was always a kitchen garden where culinary herbs were grown alongside vegetables.

The "knot garden" was developed in England in the sixteenth century. It was a complicated geometrical pattern made from two or three kinds of evergreen herbaceous plant. For preference, these were different in colour, such as box (*Buxus sempervirens*), cotton lavender (*Santolina chamaecyparissus*), and germander (*Teucrium chamaedrys*). The plants were so positioned in this design that it seemed as though they passed over and through each other wherever they met. Space left over between these evergreen patterns was planted with ground-covering herbs.

**Practical and full
of flowers**
In medieval times, the herb garden often formed a part of the kitchen garden. Herbs were grown according to type in small, separate, rectangular beds. These beds were often raised since it was realized,

Conifers trimmed into particular shapes are appropriate for gardens with a Japanese feeling.

Shrubs, foliage plants, and flowers are seen in a mixed border.

even then, that several herbs preferred a well-drained, drier soil. Paths ran between these small beds so that the appropriate herb could be found according to type. Two main paths cut through the herb garden in the form of a cross. Water could be fetched from the cistern where the paths intersected. Such a cruciform was an elementary feature. Since the use of herbs had been around for centuries, some of them were treated with great respect. Superstition played a large part. You could be virtually certain that herbaceous plants such as wormwood (*Artemisia absinthum*), and thorn apple (*Datura stramonium*) harboured the devil. Monks believed that a path in the form of a cross would put the devil to flight. These old herb gardens had flowers too. The Madonna lily (*Lilium candidum*), peony (*Paeonia officinalis*), the white lily (*Lilium regale*), hollyhocks (*Althaea rosea*), wall-flowers (*Cheiranthus cheirii*), varieties of iris, and several kinds of rose were used to decorate the church. The garden was also enlivened by the following flowers: foxgloves (*Digitalis purpurea*), marigolds (*Calendula officinalis*), lavender (*Lavandula officinalis*), soapwort (*Saponaria officinalis*), sage (*Salvia officinalis*), marjoram (*Origanum vulgare*), rosemary (*Rosmarinus officinalis*), fennel (*Foeniculum vulgare*), mallow (*Malva sylvestris*), monkshood (*Aconitum napellus*), and sweet bergamot (*Monarda didyma*). You might never have guessed now that these plants, so abundant in flowers, were all used medicinally.

Other uses Many of the well-known herbs listed above are used in the kitchen. To us, bergamot is a decorative plant. I presume that you have not given any to your son-in-law as part of your daughter's dowry, since an extract from its petals works wonders for young mothers, so they used to say.

Strong-smelling herbs were much prized in medieval kitchens. As there were few ways to preserve food, meat and milk products very often had a strange taste. By using herbs liberally in cooking, any unpleasant odours or tastes could be completely masked.

Floors were impregnated with the oils contained in lavender and rosemary. Not only did it smell pleasant but the floor would shine as well. These herbs would be strewn over carpets and mats too. Just brush in well and your fleas are gone.

At a time when sewerage was an open ditch and lavatories were just a hole in the ground, gentlemen and ladies would often walk about holding scented bouquets to their noses to prevent themselves fainting from the stench. It can be seen from this that, because of the poor sanitary conditions, herbs could not be removed from the garden. In spite of the many changes in gardening fashions, the herbs maintained their stance.

The rise of the landscape style entailed the banishment of herbs from ornamental gardens to the kitchen garden, only to return alongside the perennials towards the end of the nineteenth century; most

An old-fashioned herb garden where space has been left intentionally for a view over the park in the background.

87

herbaceous plants were then given a place in the border next to the perennials.

A walled herb garden has the advantage of trapping warmth within its walls.

Ornamental and pot plants

The terms annual, biennial, short-lived, bedding plants, and pot plants are often used together. They only really tell us about the way in which we should grow or use these plants in our climate.

If the garden styles from which they originated are analysed it can be seen that annuals and biennials, apart from being bedding plants, were also used as pot plants. Pots in Renaissance gardens were set along (not on) the axes and at the corners of parterres in such a way that their symmetry was never disrupted. Flower gardens were subordinate to the rest of the garden during the baroque. Only at the end of the seventeenth century were flower borders laid out around the *parterres de broderie*. However, at that time, annuals and biennials were arranged along the axes of these gardens in large pots.

If the annuals and biennials no longer looked respectable, or had finished flowering, they could be replaced at a moment's notice. Sufficient stock was available in the nursery areas, usually in a walled garden.

Annuals, low-growing biennials, and succulents were also used to fill up carpet beds. Like the annuals, biennials were prepared in advance in the nursery and then planted out in the flower-beds surrounding the parterres, or in pots. Taller, flowering perennials and biennials were probably cultivated in the nursery as well since these plants could provide attractive, long-lasting, cut flowers to decorate the castle or mansion.

In present-day gardens, annuals and biennials are often included in kitchen-garden plans for use as cut flowers. They are also employed in mixed borders. Annuals and biennials are ideal "gap-fillers". A disadvantage is that they wander – they do not seed themselves according to plan and will place themselves somewhere else again next year.

Scaevola *and* Petunia, *two annuals which complement each other's colours wonderfully.*

Many border plants can also be used as pot plants.

The green boundary

Marking out the terrain is the most

important aspect of laying out a new

garden. Therefore, it is often the first task

in the garden to be tackled.

Most of us want to be safeguarded against

intruders, onlookers, and the wind.

The idea of sitting somewhere exposed is unpleasant: you want to feel comfortable. The most attractive means of enclosing an area, and the one which lasts the longest, comes from the natural partition made by a hedge. Some of the most beautiful hedges are made by shrubs.

The hedges contain the ornamental garden.

From box edges to green walls

Hedging has appeared throughout the centuries, whichever garden style you look at, whether it be from the ancient Egyptians, the much more recent cottage garden style, or the present-day garden.
People have always wanted to protect and demarcate their property. In medieval times of war with knights on horseback, walls were built to surround castles and personal territory, and the space within these walls was divided further by low hedges. Almost all sections of formal gardens were enclosed by hedging.

Hedges were even used to make mazes. Incidentally, this sort of hedging was not always tall; as seen particularly in the low-lying hedges of monastery garden mazes. These were not much use to our eyes since the right path is soon spotted, yet the intention behind these mazes was, in fact, to learn discipline and, through meditation, to find the righteous path calmly by following "difficult roads".
Hedges in the Renaissance were still small scale, surrounding flower-borders, while in the baroque period they were employed to widen perspective.

The layout of the gardens at Hidcote Manor (England) in 1907 was the start of a new garden style: the compartmentalized garden. The garden there was divided into several "garden rooms", each of which could contain something completely different from the next.
Hedges usually provided the border between these separated, individual gardens.

Old hedges in new clothes

According to an old Chinese saying, "A garden without a hedge is a coat without a collar". What first comes to mind when talking about a hedge is the garden's boundary.

Indeed, even if you have only a little space, a hedge makes a beautiful boundary which can lessen or break the wind since it does not form a completely solid surface.

However, a hedge can also protect a play area or vegetable patch and a garden can be divided up in this way to create different areas each with its own function, without having the garden viewed all in one go. By using hedging like this, the garden seems bigger and more exciting: through every passageway lies another surprise.

The concept created at the end of the last century by the English garden designer Gertrude Jekyll and realized in the present-day border also included a new role for the hedge: it provided a backdrop to the border. All plants show up well against this calm expanse of

> **TIP**
> Pull up the hedge roots alongside the hedge's edge and then cut them off with a spade. Dig a trench which can then be filled with manure. Next, fill the trench with the excavated soil.

Low box hedging determines the parterre's pattern.

green and you will kill two birds, even three, with one stone because the garden will have a boundary, a wind-break, and a backdrop all at the same time.

A hedge with a tint

The advantage of a living hedge is that something different can be experienced from it in each season so long as deciduous hedging which will provide the greatest variety has been chosen. If you have some space, then a rose hedge can be very pretty – for example *Rosa rugosa* 'Alba' with its white flowers. If you prefer a hedge with an autumnal cachet then the several varieties of barberry (*Berberis*) must be considered: most of them turn fabulous colours and produce berries as well (not only the best known, which is red all year). However, they are all very prickly.

Vigorous firethorn (*Pyracantha*), hornbeam (*Carpinus betulus*), species roses, and cotoneaster (*Cotoneaster*) are individual bushes which also offer nesting to birds when planted as a loose hedge. A choice can be made from flowering shrubs, as well, when planting a loose hedge. It is true that these shrubs take up much more space and so they should be planted at greater distances from each other, which also has its financial advantages. Small box or lavender hedges fit in well with the scale of herb and kitchen gardens, or alongside rose beds.

Conditions on the spot

The intention is usually for a hedge to remain on the same spot for years. Therefore, choice of hedging should be above all determined by the soil type. After all, the idea is that your hedge should stay healthy and grow densely. That is most likely to happen if it is made to feel comfortable through good pruning and feeding.

When a border is placed alongside a hedge, a strip of ground 30–50cm (12–20in) in width should be left in between. This unpaved path is useful to walk on when the hedge needs clipping or the border needs weeding and will also provide room for feeding.

Coniferous hedging

Just looking around, it can be seen that coniferous hedging is coming back into fashion, but note that conifers grow well only in fairly sandy, peaty, or loamy soils.

The arbor vitae, *Thuja occidentalis*, is a fast, wind-proof grower that dislikes salty sea air, and does fairly well in the shade. However, it does go brown in the winter, which many people find a problem. The *Thuja* takes well to pruning and its cultivars, *Thuja occidentalis* 'Compacta Pyramidalis' which is bluish-green and *Thuja occidentalis* 'Holmstrup' which stays a deep green, are also suitable for hedging. The latter grows more slowly and will require two or so to be planted every meter (3ft). Arbor vitae becomes bare underneath when not given enough individual space in which to grow.

TIP
A slightly higher hedge around a rose or herb garden will not only keep the wind at bay, but will also keep wonderful scents trapped there.

TIP
When planting a hedge which forms a boundary with neighbours it is wise to tell them what you are planning to do before starting.

The dwarfish Lawson cypress *Chamaecyparis lawsoniana* and its various cultivars, such as *C. l.* 'Triomf van Boskoop' and 'Green Hedger', are also fairly fast growing and suitable for hedging but do not like shade at all and react badly to wind. The Lawson cypress can be lightly trimmed.

If your garden is very large and you want to sit snugly in it as soon as possible, then it is best to use *Cupressocyparis* x *leylandii*. This sturdy, fast grower retains good foliage cover underneath and is more than happy being clipped back. It can withstand sea winds and will eventually become too tall for many gardens.

The yew tree (*Taxus baccata*) concludes the list of conifers and cannot be praised highly enough. Yew makes few demands of the soil, is able to grow where they are limy and heavy, and even accepts shade. It tolerates severe pruning marvellously, even to the trunk with the only drawback being that it grows slowly and is expensive. Its foliage and berries are poisonous to man and beast alike.

Evergreen hedging   Tall, evergreen hedges which can be clipped include the prickly holly (*Ilex aquifolium*), privet (*Ligustrum ovalifolium*) which loses its leaves during hard frosts, and the cherry laurels (*Prunus lauroceracus* 'Caucasica' and *P. l.* 'Rotundifolia'). It is better to prune cherry laurels back with a pair of secateurs than to use hedge-shears. Medium-sized, evergreen hedging can be chosen from privet

This hedge demarcates the patio's boundary.

TIP

Compared with trees and shrubs, conifers have a fairly small, compact root system. That is why they are more sensitive to storms and strong winds. They are blown over at an angle (or even completely flattened) much sooner than shrubs.

93

(*Ligustrum ovalifolium*), oval-leafed hollies (*Ilex aquifolium* 'J.C. van Tol' and *I. a.* 'Laurifolia'), and firethorn (*Pyracantha coccinea* 'Orange Glow'). The holly *Ilex meservae* 'Blue Prince', with its gentle, non-spiny leaves, survives a winter excellently except in thin soil or windy positions. Low, evergreen hedging can be made from the evergreen, bushy variety of honeysuckle *Lonicera nitida*, *Ilex crenata* 'Convexa', or *Buxus sempervirens*, *B. s.* 'Suffruticosa', and *B. s.* 'Hansworthensis'. The last named has slightly larger leaves, grows faster, and is suitable for making rather larger hedges as well. Also suitable for low hedging in sheltered spots are the sub-shrub lavender (the lime-loving *Lavandula officinalis*) and its many varieties, some shrubby varieties of veronica such as *Hebe armstrongii*, and cotton lavender (*Santolina*).

A part of the garden enclosed by box hedging based on ancient Persian principles of gardening: a square cut into quarters by two crossing paths.

Evergreen, loose hedging
For this sort of hedge one should consider the barberry varieties *Berberis darwinii*, *B. gagnepainii*, *B. julianae*, and *B. stenophylla*, cotoneaster (*Cotoneaster franchetii*), the spindle tree (*Euonymus fortunei* 'Vegetus'), holly (*Ilex aquifolium*), privet (*Ligustrum quihoui*), firethorn (*Pyracantha coccinea*), and osmanthus (*Osmanthus heterophyllus*).

Deciduous hedging
Beech (*Fagus sylvatica*) is suitable for making high hedges and some of the most beautiful ones but, unfortunately, does not grow quickly.

> **TIP**
> High and low, evergreen hedging can also be made with common ivy, *Hedera helix*. Put a sturdy piece of wire mesh in place and let the ivy grow over it. Two plants are enough for every 1m (3ft) stretch.

It is well known as a former 'courtyard' plant, the courtyard in question being the kitchen garden where the garden's soil was formerly well worked in and manured. Beech grows well in light soils but is sensitive to changes in ground water and cannot tolerate sea winds well. The common hornbeam, *Carpinus betulus*, is not as heavily demanding as far as soil is concerned, nor is it deterred by wetter soils, and it makes an attractive hedge too. Hornbeam will also grow well in clay (and limy) soils.

This is a pleasant spot to sit in, protected from the wind.

The hedge maple, *Acer campestre*, can put up with truly anything.
The common privet, *Ligustrum vulgare* 'Atrovirens', is fast growing in all soil types. Its leaves are longer and narrower than those of *Ligustrum ovalifolium* but have an attractive, really green colour. Furthermore, it only sheds its leaves late in the year.

Hawthorn, *Crataegus monogyna*, does not grow well in a chemically polluted atmosphere but is otherwise extremely hardy. The cornelian cherry (*Cornus mas*), hawthorn, and mountain currant (*Ribes alpinum*) create excellent, medium-height hedging and do not mind hard pruning.
Finally, lower hedging can be made from the snowberry (*Symphoricarpus chenaultii*), the mountain currant (*Ribes alpinum*), and *Ligustrum vulgare* 'Lodense'.

TIP

Planting distances for coniferous hedging: *Thuja occidentalis*, 3 in each 1m (3ft) stretch; *Chamaecyparis lawsoniana*, 2 in each 1.5m (5ft) stretch; *Cupressocyparis* x *leylandii*, 1 in each 1m (3ft) stretch; *Taxus baccata*, 5 in each 2m (6ft) stretch.

Deciduous, loose hedging

The following should be borne in mind: the crab apple (*Malus sargentii*), the barberry (*Berberis aggregata*), the cotoneasters (*Cotoneaster divaricatus, C. dielsianus,* and *C. simonsii, Eleagnus multiflora*); forsythia (*Forsythia intermedia*), Aaron's beard (*Hypericum hookerianum*), mock orange (*Philadelphus coronarius*), potentilla (*Potentilla fruticosa*), the buckthorn (*Rhamnus frangula*), the elder (*Sambucus nigra*), and the spiraeas (*Spiraea arguta,* foam of May; *S. bumalda,* and *S. salicifolia*).

Species roses do not look at all misplaced as hedges either. The dog rose (*Rosa canina*) can put up with a shady location, first producing pink flowers followed by red rose-hips. From the petals of the similarly tall-growing sweet-brier, *Rosa rubiginosa,* comes the most delicious apple scent, this rose having pink flowers with orange-red hips. *Rosa rubrifolia* (syn. *Rosa glauca*) steals the show with its purple-grey, red-veined leaves and beautiful autumn colours. As well as the leaves, there are also small pink flowers and red hips to admire. A medium-sized rose hedge can be made using *Rosa rugosa.* This vigorous grower provides a good display even on poorer soils. Its flowers are red, and rose-hip jam can be made from the fruits.

With its dark-red hips and gorgeous autumn colours, *Rosa nitida* will create a low hedge and will even tolerate some shadow. *Rosa virginiana* 'Harvest Song', once again with pink flowers and orange-red hips, turns a breath-taking, overwhelming yellow in the autumn.

The Leyland cypress is an extremely fast grower which should really only be used if very high hedging is wanted.

Hedges delineate the garden's various sections.

Planting distances for individual hedging shrubs

Planting distances for shrubs used to make loose hedges can be taken from the shrub planting distances given in Chapter 3. However, since these shrubs are meant to form a hedge they may be planted a little closer to each other. There are other specifications for shrubs intended to form a closed wall and to become a trimmed hedge.

Plant	no. of examples in a 1m (3ft) stretch
beech, *Fagus sylvatica*	4 to 5
hornbeam, *Carpinus betulus*	4
hedge maple, *Acer campestre*	4
hawthorn, *Crataegus monogyna*	3 to 4
privet, *Ligustrum*	4
cornelian cherry, *Cornus mas*	3
mountain currant, *Ribes alpinum*	3
holly, *Ilex*	3 to 4
cherry laurel, *Prunus laurocerasus*	2 to 3
firethorn, *Pyracantha coccinea*	3
bushy honeysuckle, *Lonicera nitida*	3 to 4
box, *Buxus sempervirens*	5
lavender, *Lavandula angustifolia*	4
shrub veronica, *Hebe*	4
cotton lavender, *Santolina chamaecyparissus*	4

Privet needs pruning back often but it makes an excellent firm hedge. It doesn't mind at all where it is planted.

TIP

You might want a hedge made by osier shoots (willow) to form a partition. Stick the approximately 3.5m (12ft) long osier shoots into the ground at an angle of 45° and at a distance of 20cm (8in) from each other. Then make a second row flush with the first using the same angle but in the opposite direction. The whole thing is supported by poles and tied to them with string. It needs regular weaving and pruning. After two years it will have grown over solidly.

Pruning, shaping, and training

Western gardening ideas are influenced as much by the formal garden style which had its origins in Egypt as by the more informal style from China.

A well-pruned hedge is green from top to bottom.

While a rigid, symmetrical design belongs to the formal garden, a more natural layout is the characteristic feature of the informal, and often asymmetrical, garden.

Pruning, shaping, and training might first lead one to think about a formal garden, but trimmed shapes can also provide a framework and bring calm and order into the design of an informal garden.

Pruning

Every branch, twig, or shoot ends in a terminal bud, the growth point. A growth hormone in the bud is partially converted into a growth-inhibiting compound under the influence of light (consider the thin, hasty growth pattern of plants left in the dark). If these buds are never pruned they will subsequently develop into new shoots; the growth of buds lying further behind will be inhibited. If the terminal buds are pruned, however, growth inhibition in the lateral buds is removed and side-shoots quickly develop below the point of incision. Pruning usually occurs in ornamental, kitchen, and fruit gardens to create a good shape or to preserve a shape which already exists. Pruning also encourages better growth in developing flower buds and fruit, and it revitalizes bushes.

Flowering shrubs

In the shrubbery, and also in the mixed border, there are many bushes which will have been purchased for their distinctive flowers in particular. After a few years, the bush will have grown increasingly

large and, worse, will have started to flower more and more on its top and outer sides. Long term, the shrub will become so old that it will no longer flower at all. Since a shrub flowers most when young, it makes sense to maintain its youthfulness.

Flowering shrubs can be divided into two major groups: the spring-flowering and summer-flowering shrubs. Shrubs whose flowering season comes before 1 July will produce flowers from the wood that grew in the previous year (and the years preceding that).

Immediately after flowering, all the branches which have produced flowers should be pruned back as heavily as possible, preferably to just above ground level. The year-old stems (with no lateral branching) are left undisturbed. If only a few young shoots have sprung from the ground, then the old shoots which have finished flowering are pruned back to just above their lowest situated youngest branch. However, never cut off old branches to leave a height of 1m (3ft) or more since many new shoots will form just below your incision if you do, and the underside of the bush will become bare.

A few examples of these more or less spring-flowering shrubs are Forsythia (*Forsythia intermedia*), mock orange (*Philadelphus*), Jew's mallow (*Kerria japonica*), the spiraea bushes *Spiraea arguta* (foam of May) and *S. thunbergii*, flowering currant varieties (*Ribes*), and the tamarisk (*Tamarix tetrandra*).

Summer-flowering shrubs, with a main season after 1 July, produce

The gaps visible in the far hedge clearly show that it was incorrectly and insufficiently cut back when younger.

flowers from the shoots formed that spring and in early summer so all of their branches may be pruned back in early spring.

Aaron's beard (*Hypericum*), potentilla (*Potentilla*), and the summer-flowering bush *Spiraea bumalda* can be cut back to 10cm (4in) above ground level.

The butterfly bush (*Buddleia davidii*) and the hydrangea (*Hydrangea paniculata*) grow most from their youngest wood (wood that grew in the previous year), which is why they are often severely pruned back to form a cluster of old branches just above the ground.

Many kinds of shrub can make hedging. This photograph clearly shows that a hedge does not necessarily need to be in a straight line.

Hedges The hedging shrubs mentioned in the previous chapter were picked out because experience has taught that they tolerate frequent pruning and continue to produce new wood. The frequency with which a hedge must be pruned depends on what you want it to achieve.

If your hedge needs to be fast growing and is being well manured it will have to be cut back several times a year. Pruning stimulates growth, and so does manuring.

Hedges composed of very fast growers like privet, mountain currant, Leyland cypress, and Lawson cypress will have to be pruned back many times every year.

Remember the following as a rule of thumb: prune back once every year towards the end of summer. If the hedge still grows very fast and its tight shape is being lost then cut it back once when the new shoots have been formed at the end of May, and once more at the end of July or the beginning of August. Never prune when there is a chance of frost.

Pruning more often during initial growth

Although existing hedging has now been dealt with, and the amount of pruning necessary may not have seemed so demanding, a different pruning schedule has to be maintained in the first few years after planting a new hedge.

Fast-growing, deciduous hedges want to grow upwards and forget to produce lateral shoots, which will result in gaps soon appearing underneath if pruning only takes place once a year.

After planting, two-thirds of the shrub should be cut back; this often leaves a hedge only 20cm (8in) in height. In the second spring to follow planting, the main branches should be reduced to half their length while regular pruning should then start on the lateral branches. In the third year, a third should be pruned back from the top of the hedge, and so forth. One pruning around the end of July is usually sufficient once the hedge has reached its intended height. The evergreens *Lonicera nitida* and *Buxus sempervirens* must also be pruned back to at least half their size after planting so that good foliage cover can be produced at their base. Other fast-growing, evergreen hedgers should have two-thirds of their height pruned back after planting. In the second year no more than one-third should be

Buttresses attached to a yew hedge are quite easily achieved.

removed from the total height and from this time onwards the sides of these hedges should also be pruned back.

Hornbeam and beech produce a lot of lateral growth at their base by themselves. Two-thirds of their height should be pruned back after planting. Lateral growth should then be cut back slightly as well. The second year, prune back a third of all the new growth which has formed on the top and at the sides of the hedge. In subsequent years limit pruning to the annual performance at the end of summer.

A hedge which has already reached its desired height can be cut back in the spring, of course, but it then quickly forms new shoots and will require more frequent pruning throughout the year to maintain its set shape.

Having a climber grow over the hedge sounds like a nice idea in theory, but is not very practical. When you come to cut back the hedge in July, the climber is either still growing fast or else in flower. Furthermore, a woody-stemmed climber can damage the hedge.

Conifers and slow-growing, evergreen hedgers should be left to themselves for the first year. Trim the sides in the summer of their second year but until these hedges have reached their destined height you will not need to remove anything from the top. Once they have reached the required height it will be enough to cut them back just once a year (the Leyland cypress is an exception to this rule).

Box spheres can be shaped by hand as well.

TIP

The evergreen cherry laurel and other large-leaved hedgers are best not pruned back using shears as the cut leaves will become brown. This hedge is best maintained by using a pair of secateurs.

Topiary   The simplest topiary designs in hedging are indentations, niches, wavy upper edges, or buttresses. These architectural features can be cut into the hedge once it has reached its intended height. In the past, two rows of hedging plants were very often placed next to each other during planting. The hedge would then be sure to close in, becoming wider and more distinctive in relation to other components making up the garden. The greatest success can be achieved with shrubs which produce a lot of growth from old wood and which have been used for topiary for centuries: yew (*Taxus*), holly (*Ilex*), and box (*Buxus*) for lower, green designs. Moreover, they only need pruning back once a year. In fact most of the designs mentioned above can be clipped into the hedge by hand.

To make a buttress, add one or two extra plants at the planned spot during initial planting. Creating "windows" is a little more tricky. Seeing as the hedge has to close over above a window, you could try bending the branches in an existing hedge a little to one side, afterwards carefully squeezing a frame in between them. A section of the branches which have been pushed to one side will have to be cut away (in the middle of the window) and many will have to be tied to the sides and top of the frame where the branches will also need to be tied together. You could also set the frame on a pole at the required height and place this above the hedge so that the hedge can grow around it, but the effect will take much longer to achieve this way.

Golden privet is good for making spherical shapes. Its disadvantages are growing fast and needing to be trimmed frequently.

Next page: House and garden form a unity with each other and the environment.

T I P

There are different kinds of hop: the annual, *Humulus scandens*, sometimes called Japanese hop, and the perennial, *Humulus lupulus*.

Frames for rectangular windows are always best when attached to sturdy poles set in the hedge.

To make angles, spheres, and cones, allow several branches to grow on together in one place through the top of the hedge. If the idea is that the sphere should stand separate from the hedge then tie the branches together with plastic-coated wire or creosote twine. To make spheres, cones, and the like you can form your own shape out of wide-meshed wire netting (such frameworks can also be bought). Allow the branches to go on growing at first so they can be trimmed from the very start and then position the wire shape over the whole thing. All these designs, of course, can also be directly hand-shaped in the pot or when growing out in the open.

Topiary using one stem

Things become more difficult when you decide to make a topiary design grow out of a hedge on one stem since only one major shoot can then be allowed to grow on through. This needs to be cut off just above the mid-point of the future sphere. It is from this point that the future spheroid develops. For example, if you want to produce a sphere with a diameter of 50cm (20in) on top of a stem which is 1m (3ft) tall, then cut the main stem at a length of 1.27m (3ft 11in). Afterwards, leave all lateral branches which grow at 1m (3ft) or higher above the top of the hedge untouched. These will go to make up the sphere's underside. If you do not have a sharp eye or a steady hand for

TIP

Strong wire and bamboo sticks can also be used in shaping. The shoots growing through the openings in these frames can be pruned back a little, which will encourage lateral and faster growth.

Hawthorn lends itself well to being trimmed into a dome shape.

The chances of the upper parts of this stepped design becoming brown are minimalized because of the overall tapered style.

clipping, then create the design by once more using a frame which is firmly attached to a stick.

A dome or mushroom shape is also amongst one's options but in this case the principal shoot should be cut just below the future, uppermost part of the dome.

If a sphere is to be shaped above a stem which is in a pot or self-standing in the open, its main shoot (the future stem) should never be pruned completely bare during its growing period. The main shoot will lengthen every year and produce lateral growth which should be trimmed back a bit in the spring. The following spring, lateral shoots growing from new upward growth should be cut back slightly but the growth below that should be ignored. Lateral shoots which were pruned back slightly one year earlier can be cut right back to the stem.

The distance separating such topiary steps must be enough to allow sufficient light to reach the upper surfaces. These upper sections will otherwise turn brown.

Topiary done in stages and animals

A fir-cone shape made up of staggered stages is not so difficult to create. Many evergreens can be used for this. A complete fir-cone shape is grown first, and afterwards comes the pruning. Before trimming starts, it must be decided first whether or not this bush should be set on a plinth. This would in fact make it more distinctive. Firstly, trim the plinth into the desired shape and then, starting at the top of the plinth, cut off all lateral branches from the main stem up to a height of 30cm (12in). This is the shaping of the first stage. You may notice that the branches rise at an angle to the stem. These need to be

TIP

It is quite possible to have another species of shrub growing along with the rest of the hedge and later to shape a dome, cone, or sphere from it, once the hedge has reached its intended height.

bent down to the horizontal and tied tightly to the stem underneath with plastic-coated wire or creosote twine. The second stage should then come about 30cm (12in) above the first, and so forth.

The lowest branches from the next stage above must be bent down and secured each time to create a horizontal plane. The cone shape needs to taper clearly from ground level to its apex: each stage should be given a smaller diameter. The underside of each stage will always be bare as no light will be able to penetrate, but the upper surface of the stages will stay green so long as the gaps between the stages have been cut out correctly and each higher stage is smaller than the last.

A cone-shaped bush can also be used to make a spiral, *Taxus* and *Buxus* once more being the shrubs with a proven track record for this. However, the most attractive results will be achieved when the spiral shape is clipped into the bush during its growth.

Topiary animals can be best shaped and clipped from slightly older conifers or from evergreen shrubs with small leaves, the ideal plants again being *Buxus* and *Taxus*. An animal set on a plinth or grown in a pot comes across better than one grown from a self-standing bush at ground level. Clipping by hand is extremely tiresome: your animal's progress will have to be kept under control by training it along string and then cutting in. Therefore make an animal out of wire-mesh netting first or, even better, from strong metal wire. Choose an animal with a clear profile such as a swan (its neck), a rabbit (its ears), or a

A spiral requires a good feeling for shape and a steady hand when clipping.

bird (its tail-feathers and wings), and add no other details to the shape. Just as with the simpler designs, allow one shoot (where there is to be one stem) or more to grow through the hedge plinth. The wire-frame guide should then be fixed on to a secure pole in the middle of the plinth. Allow a few shoots to go on growing upwards. These are then tied up together with creosote twine or plastic-coated wire and trained around the outside of the wire-frame. A few shoots will also grow within the wire-frame and will need to be pruned back to stimulate the growth of lots of lateral branches. The shape can be steadied in a pot by using bamboo sticks.

Some bushes and trees have a naturally rounded shape, such as the false acacia (*Robinia pseudoacacia* 'Umbraculifera'), *Prunus fruticosa*, the maple (*Acer platanoides* 'Globosum'), and the bushy ivies (*Hedera helix* 'Arborescens' and *H. colchica* 'Arborescens') which only need to be pruned back a little. Particularly with reference to trees, this pruning is done in one of two ways. There is pollarding, where all the branches are pruned back hard to just above the stem, but this does result in having to look at a strangely knotted lump for several months. Alternatively, one branch can be cut back to the stem while the next one is only pruned to half its length, and so on. This alternate pattern will at least give you a framework to look at in the winter months.

Left: Perfect topiary squirrels set upon equally perfect topiary plinths.

Clipped animal shapes receive more attention when placed on a plinth.

Evergreen seats   If you can make a topiary animal then making a topiary garden seat or chair will be no problem at all. A plank set on top of a few concrete blocks can easily serve as a seat. Concrete U-shaped blocks are ideal for this purpose. Decide in advance what you find a comfortable height to sit at and then place the seat in the garden, planting either evergreen bushes or slow-growing conifers along the sides and back. These need to have a naturally upward growth pattern. The front of the seat can also be flanked by greenery if this is desired, but make sure that the seat does not go too far back.

By pruning back regularly in the first few years, the arm and back-rests will grow up quickly. It will not provide real support, of course, but when supplemented with a cushion a seat like this is more than tolerable.

These false acacias really look very odd when pruned back this way.

Trees   Lime trees supported by stakes are often used in making screens or espaliers. However, it is also quite possible to use plane, elm, horse chestnut, or maple. Since these trees all have good regenerative powers they take well to being trained and repeatedly pruned.

A trim avenue of limes   The limes *Tilia platyphyllos*, *Tilia* x *vulgaris* 'Pallida', and *Tilia* x *vulgaris* 'Black Lime' are those most used as standards for training. *Tilia euchlora*, which is sometimes recommended as a training lime, has rather strongly downward-hanging branches which will involve a

TIP

Give your topiary shapes space. The majority of evergreens are quite happy when planted in isolation. They hate being squashed up against other plants and old clippings. Leaves which are covered up like this will discolour and die through lack of light.

lot of intervention if a formal design is required. It has one big advantage in not being prone to aphid infestation.

There are several ways in which a lime can be trained. The most well known are the palmate espalier and the hedge form. Palmate espaliers are very strictly trained and more or less symmetrical in design. The branches are trained to lie on a horizontal plane. A variation known as the oblique palmate is where branches are grown at something of an upward angle to the tree-trunk. The hedge form is theoretically just a free shape maintained like a hedge.

In the sixteenth and seventeenth centuries, these strictly trained trees were used to form high screens both within and surrounding gardens. These screens acted like stage wings and determined the garden's boundaries. If you would like to make your own lime espalier it is recommended that trees be chosen with a trunk circumference of at least 14–16cm (6in) measured from 3ft above ground level. It is then possible to start shaping several levels immediately. Plant the trees 2.7–6.6m (8–11ft) distance from each other depending on the height of the first level and the length of your "lime avenue". The branches from each tree can be trained along a bamboo frame, but it is better to tie them along a taut wire rail. The wires should be stretched between stakes set in the ground. The height of the stakes depends on the height of your uppermost layer of branches. In the main, wires are stretched at intervals of about 40cm (16in), one above the other.

Not expensive garden furniture, but a seat made from clipped box.

Bend down two opposite branches where the lowest level is to begin, and secure them along the wire rail with plastic-coated wire. A further 40cm (16in) up select another two branches which lie close to the wire rail and bend these down. Two more branches should be attached to the next wire rail 40cm (16in) above this. Should you run out of branches to use for the following level, cut the main stem of the tree just above the lateral shoots from the last level. New branches will grow below this incision point in the following year, when you will be able to attach them to the wires to make the next level. The remaining branches between levels can be cut from the tree's trunk.

A charming little bower can be made from wisteria with just a little support.

Pruning and training limes

How you then tackle pruning depends on the style you want to create. Do you only want separate layers of foliage with spaces in between, or do you one day want a completely closed screen? Must it become a flat screen, or do you want to create more substantial growth? Some general tips follow on shaping and maintaining trained limes.

The branches' ends must point slightly upwards during shaping in order to maintain growth in the trained branches. Their terminal shoots should never be pruned as long as the trained branches are still growing towards each other. Every winter, long lateral shoots may be pruned back or even removed from the trained branches. Any short lateral shoots are left alone. Laterals will grow faster the closer they are to the tree's main stem, which is where the hardest pruning needs

TIP

If you are able to fix lime branches to all of your wire rails in one go, then the best way to proceed with the uppermost level is to bend down just one lateral branch onto one wire rail and next to bend down the main stem onto the other rail to be used like a lateral shoot.

to take place. The lowest rail will tend to grow more slowly so its lateral shoots should be pruned back less. Growth on the lowest rail can be stimulated by cutting back more of the vertically growing lateral shoots from rails higher up. Shoots which have grown downwards from the rails do not need pruning as they will make very little growth. Eventually, the branches which have started touching those from other trees can be allowed to grow into each other.

Once this living framework has established itself, the trained lime trees can be clipped like a hedge, but they will not produce as much lateral wood as does hornbeam, for example.

Other shapes using trees

A bower of trees should not create the impression of a dark tunnel, so width should usually be kept to about 2.5m (8ft), while the height should be about 1.5 x the width. Some kind of supporting structure will be needed, such as arches and crossbeams. Wood looks most natural and iron is more expensive, of course. Wisteria (*Wisteria floribunda*) – first trained up a pole before forming a roof – and London plane trees (*Platanus acerifolia*) can be used. Six branches are usually chosen (major branches from the crown of the tree) and are trained flat against a horizontal frame. All shoots growing upwards are cut off in winter. Laterally growing shoots are trained as much as possible from rail to rail to make a sort of spider's web. Shoots which are growing too vertically can be removed in summer too.

TIP

Try planting cordon apples against a fence. If the apple's main stem is planted at an oblique angle of 45°, very strong growth will be stimulated and the stem will start bearing fruit very early in life. Blossom can be enjoyed in spring, followed by fruit in summer and autumn. Prune in winter as well as in summer.

A hornbeam canopy grown with standard trees.

Vertical lines

There has always been a need to mark out a garden. This was first done using walls and embankments.

Depending on the time and the culture in which a garden was laid out, these walls were put to ever more decorative use, sometimes using ornamentation, and sometimes using climbing plants.

A vine enjoys the warmth from a wall but does need plenty of space.

As well as this, people kept bringing more vertical structures into the garden. Originally intended as supports to train climbing fruit trees, and as shade from the sun, these were later also used for other purposes. This is how trellises, arbour retreats, arches, tunnels, and pergolas originated. Nowadays, these structures are used a great deal in gardens. Even in gardens where there is little space, where there is not always room for individual trees, they can offer us the shelter of a roof and set our gaze upward, beyond the garden boundary.

Walls Walls are universal. At one time, they were principally erected to bar animals, and in times of war and unrest people sought refuge within them. A vegetable garden could always be found inside a wall. Even if the gates had been closed shut for months people were assured of food.

The Persians introduced glazed tiling to their walls and variations in brickwork, while the Romans placed structures such as pinnacles, spheres, pineapples, and vases on top. In China, walls were given open, round windows: the gates of the moon. The circle was the symbol for heaven. In the eighteenth century, zigzag walls became popular in colder areas since the recessed parts of such walls offered extra shelter to the plants growing there. These included exotics such as figs and vines which could be grown to bear sumptuous fruit. Sometimes smoke chambers were even built into walls so that when a

wood fire was lit its smoke would pass through these chambers and provide the walls with extra warmth.

A walled garden is distinctive in possessing an individual prevailing climate and in its near total restriction of noise from outside. Unfortunately, natural stone cannot always be used anywhere we happen to be, and building a brick wall can also be rather expensive these days. One word of comfort, almost all of us have a wall which may serve some other purpose: the garden shed, the garage, or, failing that, the wall of the house. This is usually a fairly high wall which can offer many planting possibilities. Shed or garage walls are mostly lower, but suitable plants can be found for these locations as well.

Heat absorption Brick and stone absorb heat throughout the day and gradually release this at night. West and south-facing walls are, therefore, ideal locations for plants requiring a little extra warmth – such as roses, fruit trees, and a number of plants whose hardiness may be in doubt like the various evergreen varieties of *Ceanothus*. The best plants for wall growth are bushy climbers, or bushes which can be trained to climb by pruning, their branches thus benefiting from the irradiated warmth. A bush's root ball should not be placed too close to a wall as this is where the poorest soil lies, being a mixture of rubble, bricks, and pure sand. Plants will often receive no water when placed squarely up against a wall, sometimes because the roof overhangs

Fruit trees, in particular, benefit from the warmth radiated by a wall.

115

Walls shelter the plants next to them.

slightly. Moreover, plants will be unable to form a well-spread root system since their roots will all be forced in the direction of the garden. The root ball is most sensibly placed 50cm (20in) from the wall to overcome any disadvantages for the roots.

North and east-facing house walls give out warmth in winter (from central heating) and are suitable for forest climbing plants such as ivy (*Hedera*) and the Japanese climbing hydrangea (*Hydrangea petiolaris*).

Walls have just one disadvantage: they do not allow the wind through. If wind hits a wall square on, there will be resulting damage in all directions. The space between houses can often act like a wind tunnel but the wind's strength can be broken and filtered out by planting shrubs and trees in front of this area and dotted about within it.

Giving climbing plants something to climb

The majority of climbers and creepers need something to which they can cling in order to climb upwards. Many ivies (varieties of *Hedera*), Japanese climbing hydrangea (*Hydrangea petiolaris*), trumpet creeper (*Campsis radicans*), and Virginia creeper (varieties of *Parthenocissus*) attach themselves by means of suckers or adhesive roots. In the first year after planting it will seem as though they have no idea which way to grow, and will have to be directed by you towards and against the wall. Afterwards, everything will take its

TIP

Some climbers, such as *Clematis*, naturally grow upwards towards the sunlight from shady positions. The flowers also need sunlight in the majority of varieties. The optimal growing situation is in a border where *Clematis* is allowed to grow over shrubs rather than up against a wall.

The trumpet creeper is a fast climber for a warm, sunny spot.

natural course and the only things left to do will be the pruning back and thinning out.

Other climbers have winding stems with trailing tendrils and leaves and need something around which they can entwine, whereas trained plants are always dependent on some kind of support. In almost all cases, trained plants need horizontal *and* vertical support, demands which lattice-work trellises or reinforced-steel frames meet completely. Fix the supporting structure about 5cm (2in) from the wall, which will enable shoots to wind themselves effortlessly round it and will maintain air circulation (see also under roses in Chapter 4). Setting up supports this way also eases the annual task of pruning and training, and gives access to the wall or fence if repair work is needed.

Fences

Wood, a perishable option

A water channel, wire fencing, or boscage can form your boundary if you are amongst the lucky few whose garden overlooks the countryside or who have no neighbours within sight, but should a partitioning wall not be an option then the only choice left in gardens up to medium size is a fence or hedge. People usually want their gardens to have a solid barrier as quickly as possible. Sometimes the choice is quickly made when people find out about the Leyland cypress' growth rate and that it has to be cut back regularly to keep it in shape. It is going to be a wooden fence!

This effect is, unfortunately, almost impossible to achieve in many places, owing to the lack of a suitably sloping site, owing to the paucity of hilly terrain.

TIP

To prevent climbers from strangling themselves the shoots should be tied to a supporting structure only a few weeks after planting. The soil and the plant will then have time to establish themselves.

117

Lattice-work   Vines were being trained over wooden supports by the Persians and Egyptians as early as 2000 B.C. These upwardly trained vines and their overhanging branches offered shade, which quickly led to the supporting structure being extended to include a roof. These were in fact, the first arbours.

The great walls which encircled castles and communities remained necessary for a long time, but the space within such heavily populated areas was partitioned using less sturdy materials. Low fences, made from strips of wood in a diamond pattern, separated the various parts of a garden such as the orchard, kitchen garden, and vineyard.

In urban gardens, where people lived in close proximity to one another, arbour retreats were built. These were small, self-contained houses, partially open to the garden, with lattice-work roofs and sides. This was a place to which one could retire far from prying eyes.

These lattice-work constructions came to Europe from the Greeks and Romans but only after 1300 did they increase in aesthetic value since up until then trellises had served only practical functions. Decorative supports for roses were produced as well as large arbour retreats.

Many low, lattice-work constructions which added to and reinforced the garden's symmetry appeared in gardens during the Middle Ages and the Renaissance. For example, pergolas were built, to look like covered arcades open on one side. Animal and flower motifs

TIP

You don't have much space but still want differently shaped, clipped designs? Cut out a pattern from wide-meshed wire netting and fix it to the wall. Then grow ivy over it.

An additional wooden trellis will make wall maintenance much easier.

The windows in the lattice-work will provide light and a view once this shaded walk has been fully grown over.

decorated the supporting standards to which the lattice-work panels were attached while the crossbeams in these arbours and tunnels began to be made into arches.

The Netherlands became renowned for lattice-work in the seventeenth century. Tunnels were built with especially close-fitting lattice which was thereby able to support a large quantity of heavy growth. Lattice-work became increasingly used to divide the garden into smaller compartments. The lattice-work obelisk was particularly popular because it accentuated the vertical against the garden's level surfaces. In France, trellis construction also reached its peak in the seventeenth century and was raised to a decorative art form alongside architecture. Decorative lattice-work from the seventeenth century is also known as *treillage* to differentiate it from the much simpler trellis.

Trick perspectives

Trellis-work placed against walls was frequently used for *trompe l'œil* (deceiving the eye). A trick perspective which is now rather difficult to re-create was built into the lattice-work. The best effect is achieved when diverging lines become narrow in reality. The simplest design is with a gate or open door, giving the suggestion that the garden is much bigger than it is. A painting can be incorporated into this space, or a mirror which, in reflecting back your own garden, will make it appear larger.

The Dutch were already master-builders of lattice-work tunnels in the 17th century.

TIP

Consider giving your trellis a colour. Dark green is a safe colour that has been used for centuries. It was customary in 17th-century Holland to paint trellises blue. Obelisks were painted white.

119

The rise of the English landscape style brought with it criticism concerning lattice-work. It was considered too artificial and did not fit in with an environment where only natural features were valued. Although the need for trellises remained present in some gardens, they were largely relegated to the kitchen garden.

The Far East provided a new source of inspiration and a pagoda set in the landscape was favoured by many. The trellis tradition was restored in the nineteenth century when many pergolas, arbour retreats, and arches were erected in smaller gardens. High arches in the foreground allowed the eye enough room to wander towards the landscape laid out beyond.

New supporting structures

Flowering plants and shrubs were seen to have a more important garden role in the nineteenth century and were placed in the foreground, where trellises became the supports which they needed. Gardening slowly became a hobby for townspeople as well. Their gardens were smaller and this territory came to be bordered by trellises while within it lattice-work would separate the ornamental garden from the kitchen garden. All lattice-work was rampantly grown over by climbers and was again being fixed to walls, the most important function of which was to provide support for the climbers. Free-standing lattice-work in the garden was especially advised for roses since air could then circulate freely around them. Rustic styles

A trellis for training plants against a wall is always to be recommended.

were popular; trellis-work made of unplaned or roughly sawn wood was used to make garden furniture and partitions. Even trees were sometimes employed as supporting standards for a pergola. This period saw the application of many different styles and materials such as cast and wrought iron. These were used on their own or else combined with lattice-work to form a complete structure. All the structures used in gardens up until then were also copied in metal.

In the twentieth century a lot of emphasis has been placed on pergolas. Lattice-work is combined with more expensive materials such as stone and brick, the supports being mortared together, with wooden beams positioned above these sturdy standards.

A modern trellis adaptation.

Present-day adaptations

Trellises can be bought ready-made today, and for those who cannot wait for an open trellis to become grown over there is a choice of ready-made sections of fencing, wickerwork screens, planking, square and round poles, and logs. Attractive partitions can be made from bamboo and rush matting, too, although these materials have a short life expectancy. Simple trellis screens can be added to this list which, when combined with poles, beams, and slats, can be used to create your own garden structures. The open nature of lattice-work is its big advantage since you have only to cut the greenery back to the woodwork to gain a view outside the garden.

If the wall between you and your neighbour is too low and can be

Statuary has occupied gardens throughout the ages. Whether influenced by the times or otherwise.

121

A charmingly designed ornamental trellis provides support to climbing plants.

raised using trellis-work its appearance will not only be much gentler but will also prevent the claustrophobic feeling which a brick wall can give to a small garden.

The wood in the vertical supports which hold up a trellised wall or fence should be strong and durable, as should the materials making the corner brackets for pergolas which connect the standards with crossbeams.

Tropical hardwoods are durable but are not recommended from an environmental point of view since tropical forest has to be felled to produce it. Compacted, treated wood will last many years, or you could treat wood yourself with a preservative (annually) but the durability of the wood will then be shorter term. A collapsing fence which needs to thrown away is in effect a form of pollutant and could be called chemical waste because of the amount of chemicals with which the wood has been treated. Fortunately, the development of environment-friendly wood preservatives and paints is in full progress, and linseed-oil based products are already on the market.

This solid, wooden fence has been made less overbearing by varying its height.

The arbour retreat or summer-house

Many of the structures which add charm to gardens are built to provide shade from the sun and to hold back the wind. Too much sun is not really a problem associated with north-western Europe yet ideas have been borrowed, nonetheless, from countries where sun and heat are avoided as much as possible. The history of arbour retreats and pergolas stems from the gardening past in Egypt and Persia: countries where it can be extremely hot and where dust and sand can be blown into the garden by desert winds. All structures put up in such gardens were meant to offer shelter from sun and sandstorms, as well as creating the coolest environment possible. What was at first used to provide vines with support was expanded to make a roofed structure which was the first real arbour. Such arbours first stood on the grass but were later given tiled floors.

In the Renaissance, brick was used as well as wood for the standards supporting the trellis and was afterwards beautifully painted. Niches built into walls served as arbour retreats when roofed over, and arbours were, in fact, made from all kinds of materials. The ones made from cast and wrought iron were spectacular, and in a wet climate offered more strength and durability than wooden trellis-work did.

Arbour retreats, or summer-houses, became madly popular in the eighteenth and nineteenth centuries and were sometimes placed in a corner of the garden, partially open, as a shelter into which one could quietly retire for a while. They might otherwise be positioned where paths crossed, preferably in the middle of the garden, where the construction would be much more open with four gateways to enable free access. Such retreats tended to be all overgrown with roses.

At the end of the eighteenth century the romantic spirit swept into the

TIP

Train climbers up a trellis-work frame when planted next to a preservative-impregnated fence. The frame can then be moved away with the plants, which is useful when maintaining the fence annually .

These sturdy, mortared standards provide sufficient support for the "roof's" wooden crossbeams.

garden. A garden had to call up all manner of moods: from tranquil and cheerful to awe-inspiring, bucolic, melancholic, and picturesque. People became influenced by the Chinese and Japanese landscape style in which these kinds of moods could be evoked by all sorts of garden constructions. Summer-house retreats turned into hermitages, Chinese pagodas, and medieval chapels.

Ivy will grow anywhere.

In wetter climates, the need to have better shelter from the rain provided the arbour retreat with its roof, transforming it into more of a summer-house. Nowadays, nostalgia for all former styles of arbour retreat is becoming increasingly prevalent. Metal wire and rolled steel tubing have enabled more refinement in the design of summer-houses and their roofs which, along with arches, can now be purchased ready-made.

Pergolas and tunnels

A pergola is a foliage-covered walkway which was originally intended to support vines and which has since then evolved into a passageway or path intended to lead somewhere. It can form the link between important areas in a garden or provide a boundary, but it always leads somewhere. Pergolas give the impression of being enclosed and yet are open structures nonetheless. One very important advantage they have is to bring height into the garden. Within this leafy walkway, where light and shadow constantly play with each other, the eye is led to the light at the end of the tunnel.

Pergolas have been employed in the garden styles of all periods. They were usually made of wood or else combined with brickwork, but their construction was always solid, the supporting standards, crossbeams, and linear beams needing to be sturdy, not only to support the construction but also to bear the weight of all the climbing plants.

Personal taste and space dictate how far apart the standards should be placed lengthways. Standards spaced closely together soon create a tunnel-like impression. A tunnel is a pergola where the standards are close together and is usually made from metal. While a pergola's roof is usually made from wood and flat, a tunnel's is usually curved. Height, width, and length of pergolas depend on the amount of space available, and do not forget that taller people must be able to walk upright through them while leaves and branches will also be hanging down from above. A pergola is not a success if you can only just manage to walk along it, and this applies equally to the width.

The sides of a tunnel are much more densely overgrown, making minute attention to measurements even more important. Although bushes or creepers can be planted as close to each other as you like in tunnels, I would recommend leaving as much space between them as possible to allow light to dapple through the foliage since people can see little enough in a tunnel as it is. Tunnels usually have just one kind of plant forming the cover, for example an avenue of laburnum

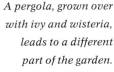

A pergola, grown over with ivy and wisteria, leads to a different part of the garden.

This pergola, which supports a vine and shades a terrace below it, is known as a loggia.

(*Laburnum anagyroides* 'Vossii'), hornbeam (*Carpinus betulus*), or holly (*Ilex*).

Laburnum trees need to be pruned and trained to create the right shape over iron arches.

Climbers   Pergolas offer many opportunities to climbing plants and bushes that can be trained, which often results in a mixture of cover. Recently, a combination of roses with clematis has become extremely popular.

The simplest tunnels are gateways or arches which were once exclusively used for entrances to gardens and houses, but which quickly became variously employed in creating vista windows or links between different sections of the garden. These could be made of wood, iron, or brick and were ornamental in design. The materials used were in keeping with other garden structures, as seen in cottage gardens where a few iron arches over which roses were usually grown functioned as a gateway. Gateways like this can be added to smaller modern-day gardens easily, while an archway set in the hedge invites a natural curiosity to know what lies on the other side!

Heavy and light planting   Climbing plants for trellises, pergolas, arbours, and summer-houses should be chosen with great care. Delicate trellis-work only requires light growth for it to become noticed in its surroundings. If a trellis has been put up to screen off some ugly walls then fast-growing climbers can be allowed to invade it. The most sensible course in this situation is to attach some kind of reinforced-steel frame to the wall.

If trellis requires regular staining treatment it is best to choose climbers which can be pruned back each spring so that cover is temporarily removed from the lattice-work and the wood can be reached. Climbing roses which flower from wood one year old should have their stems preserved, which will entail detaching them, laying them on the ground, and then re-attaching them afterwards.

A sturdy, stable summer-house can support quite a lot of growth, as can robust pergolas and walls where climbers and creepers are growing too tall up against a neighbour's fence.

Some suitable climbers

The Chinese gooseberry (*Actinidia chinensis*) needs the space provided by a pergola. It has decorative, heart-shaped leaves and requires a fair amount of warmth in order to produce fruit in quantity, which will only happen if both male and female kinds are planted together. Its smaller cousin, *Actinidia kolomikta*, with its broader, heart-shaped leaves, is a suitable climber for trellises since it does not grow as tall. The tip of the leaf is a creamy white or pink but this attractive foliage will only be produced in sunny, sheltered locations and is thus suitable for the patio garden.

Akebia quinata is somewhere in between. Its very decorative five-leafleted form entwines itself like honeysuckle, often producing a lot of bushiness above and rather less striking purplish-brown flowers in the spring. It is also suitable for a north-facing wall.

A simple yew archway permits a view behind the screening hedge.

Dry-stone walls are a perfect home for plants brought by the wind.

Many varieties of *Ampelopsis* will produce rampant growth. They have attractive, deeply divided leaves. One slightly less rampant kind, which is therefore more suitable for trellises, is *Ampelopsis brevipedunculata* 'Elegans', which has small, irregularly lobed, variegated leaves that are flecked pink and white. The young petioles and stems are red. This *Ampelopsis* requires a sheltered spot with gentle shade.

Dutchman's pipe, *Aristolochia durior*, grows massively. It has pretty, heart-shaped leaves similar to *Catalpa* which will tolerate shade, and it is splendid for forming a tunnel or a pergola – although, sadly, it is not evergreen.

Berchemia racemosa has beautifully veined, egg-shaped leaves, and after an unspectacular flowering can produce fruits which turn from green to red and then black. This will grow in a more controlled manner than *Aristolochia durior*.

The evergreen *Ceanothus* x *lobbianus* is hardy in sheltered positions, its blue flowers being a real asset for trellises.

Climbing bittersweet, *Celastrus orbiculatus*, is not suitable for trellises but does have a lovely yellow autumn colour and striking fruits (on female plants when planted together with a male plant) which turn orange-yellow.

Steadily growing plants for semi-shade and sun are *Clematis alpina* and its cultivars. They flower from April to May and should be pruned afterwards. *Clematis* 'Huldine' produces mauve-tinted white flowers in summer and is fast growing. *Clematis macropetala* and its cultivars grow to a height of 3m (10ft) and bloom from April to May. They have small flowers and attractively bearded seed heads. *Clematis montana* and its cultivars will be recognized by everyone as the familiar spring-flowering clematis and grow extremely tall, being therefore more suitable for pergolas. *Clematis viticella* and its cultivars are more restrained, can be pruned back hard in the spring, and make good trellis climbers. This plant always needs to have its feet in the shade but its flowering stems will grow towards the sun. *Clematis rehderiana* is another fast-grower which should not be left out. It has deliciously scented, bell-shaped, greenish-white flowers in late summer and attractive leaves as well, which makes for a very fragrant canopy under which to walk or sit. Reaching a height of 5m (16ft), it is also a nice plant to have climbing up a tree.

Ivy, *Hedera helix*, in all shapes and sizes, will grow rampantly on a trellis and is evergreen. It is useful for quickly providing solid cover in sun or shade.

The common hop, *Humulus lupulus*, is another rampantly growing plant and its leaves are as attractive as its bell-shaped hops.

Winter-flowering jasmine, *Jasminum nudiflorum*, is a bush which can be trained and kept well under control against a trellis. It produces yellow flowers in winter but does need disciplining with the pruning shears.

Opposite page:
A gateway is created by allowing a few shoots from the hornbeam hedge to continue growing and then weaving them together at the right height above the path.

The Japanese climbing hydrangea, *Hydrangea petiolaris*, is not very fast growing at first but needs a lot of space once established.

A very nice honeysuckle which does not grow too wildly is *Lonicera japonica* 'Aureoreticulata' which has yellow veined leaves and is also suitable for lattice-work.

Many varieties of vine (*Vitis*) which are specially grown for their leaves, and varieties of Virginia creeper (*Parthenocissus*) can be best used for pergolas or summerhouses. Creepers also prefer planting in sunny positions.

The many varieties of wisteria are stunning in combination with summer-houses and pergolas, and against high walls.

There is more than enough choice with roses. Just go to a garden centre in the flowering season and there will be many suitable varieties to consider for training against lattice-work.

There are various climbing plants amongst the annuals, almost all of which require a warm, sunny spot, such as black-eyed Susans (*Thunbergia elata*), orange petals with a chocolate-brown centre, and *Mina lobata* with its orange-yellow flowers. *Plumbago capensis* can be wintered indoors and has pale-blue flowers.

Nasturtiums, including the annual (*Tropaeolum majus*) as well as the perennial (*Tropaeolum speciosus*), are also suitable for lattice-work, but even light frosts can kill them so they will need protection in the winter.

Shrubs give a garden its "expression".

Nostalgic features in gardens nowadays

Gardens with traditional features have remained popular through the centuries – more intensely so in some periods than in others. In this chapter, "nostalgic" features are applied to gardens.

A view along the broad lateral axis.

A sumptuously flowered formal garden (see page 134)

The front garden in the diagram on page 134 belongs to an old house on the outskirts of a village. The garden was completely overgrown with conifers. The residents found the concept of a new garden layout which was completely open to the road rather worrying. They very much wanted a garden with clear axes and flower-beds, rather like a cottage garden but with straight lines.

A screen of lime trees *Tilia* x *vulgaris* 'Pallida' has been placed in a beech hedge to form the boundary, so that when walking through the garden it is rather like being inside a show-box looking back out through the peep-holes. The hedge reaches a height of about 1.4m (4ft) while the lowest lime branches start at a height of about 2.1m (6ft). The entrance to the garden and front door has been widened next to the gravel drive so there can be no doubt that this is the path leading to the house. The paving is made of concrete but in the style of brick. Passing under the limes into the garden, one looks along the central axis towards the arbour retreat, made of steel tubing and netting. The arbour is planted with ivy and will become completely overgrown in its third summer.

In the beds either side are two cone-shaped shrubs topped with spheres, *Ceanothus thyrsiflorus* var. *repens*. These evergreens, which are in fact more spreading than upward growing, have been coerced into the right shape by pruning and weaving together. A third such topiary shape plus *Lonicera japonica* 'Halliana' provide an evergreen

Planting

A formal garden

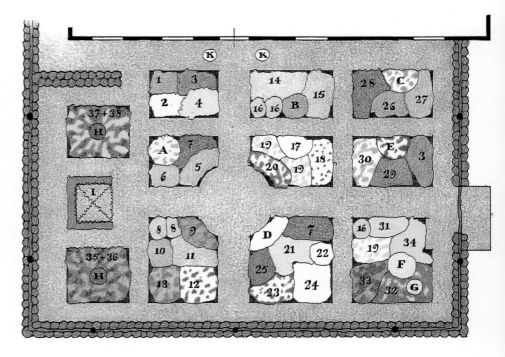

A   *Abelia grandiflora*

B   *Rubus thibetanicus*
    'Silver Fern', ornamental
    bramble

C   *Lavatera* 'Barnsley'

D   *Rosa* 'Snow Ballet'

E   *Nandina domestica*

F   *Rosa* 'Sally Holmes'

G   *Lonicera japonica*
    'Halliana', honeysuckle

H   *Ceanothus thyrsiflorus*
    var. *repens*

I   The arbour is completely grown
    over by a small-leafed ivy

K   Two large pots containing lime
    trees, *Tilia cordata*
    'Green Spire'

1   *Geranium psilostemon*, cranesbill

2   *Aster divaricatus*, aster

3   *Nepeta sibirica*, species of catmint

4   *Helleborus argutifolius*,
    Corsican Christmas rose

5   *Acaena affinis*, New Zealand burr

6   *Geranium endressii* 'Wargrave Pink',
    cranesbill

7   *Heuchera micrantha* 'Palace Purple'

8   *Euphorbia amygdaloides* var.
    robbiae, euphorbias

9   *Epimedium youngianum* 'Roseum',
    barrenwort

10 *Geranium endressii*, cranesbill

11 *Artemisia absinthium* 'Lambrook
    Silver'

12 *Salvia sclarea*, clary

13 *Centranthus ruber*, red valerian

14 *Anemone tomentosa* 'Robustissima',
    anemone

15 *Geranium pratense*
    'Mrs Kendall Clark'

16 *Euphorbia* x *martinii*

17 *Veronicastrum virginicum album*

18 *Anemone japonica* 'Honorine Jobert',
    anemone, *Dictamnus albus*, the
    burning bush, and *Lychnis coronaria*
    (preferably white), campion

19 *Rudbeckia purpurea* 'White Lustre',
    coneflower

20 *Geranium renardii*, cranesbill

21 *Euphorbia amygdaloides* 'Purpurea'

22 *Clematis recta* (planted in a pot to
    control growth)

23 *Gaura lindheimeri* 'Whirling
    Butterflies'

24 *Crambe cordifolia*, sea-kale family

25 *Veronica longifolia* 'Bauriesin'

26 *Campanula lactiflora* 'Loddon Anna',
    species of bell flower

27 *Verbena bonariensis*, verbena

28 *Rudbeckia purpurea*, coneflower

29 *Helleborus orientalis abschasicus*
    'Early Purple'

30 *Polygonum campanulatum*, species
    of knotweed

31 *Salvia officinalis* 'Icterina',
    yellow-leafed sage

32 *Cephalaria gigantea*

33 *Foeniculum vulgare* 'Giant Bronze',
    fennel

34 *Sisirynchium striatum*

35 *Geranium macrorrhizum* 'Album',
    cranesbill

36 *Astrantia major* 'Rubra',
    masterwort

37 *Alchemilla mollis*, lady's mantle

38 *Epimedium rubrum*, barrenwort

effect in the opposite corner on the street side of the garden. One principal colour has been chosen for each flower-bed and they all include a number of evergreen, foliage plants while here and there, in strategic places, somewhat taller plants have been incorporated. This prevents a view into the garden from outside. The garden is framed by *Fagus sylvatica* and *Tilia* x *vulgaris* 'Pallida'.

A view over the garden.

A herb garden on sandy soil (see page 136)

A good place to make a herb garden (diagram on page 136) lay in front of the henhouse in what used to be the kitchen garden. The old fruit trees were left standing, as was the boundary on the south-western side. A path made of concrete tiles, sized 30 x 30cm (12 x 12in) and 40 x 60cm (16 x 24in), runs from behind the garage, right through the herb garden, under the rose archway, and so on to the ornamental garden. Side paths ensure that herbs can be reached whatever the weather. A small pond with duckweed (VII) recalls wells in herb gardens from the past. Turf has been laid down around the pond edge on which bugle, creeping Jenny, and *Filipendula hexapetala* are growing. Many old-fashioned flowering plants, known to old herb gardens, are also in amongst the kitchen herbs.

A box border behind the cottage (see page 138)

A small, formal flower garden (diagram on page 138) lies just behind the cottage, making up one part of this large cottage garden's generally informal layout. The east side is a little more in shadow than

135

Planting

A herb garden on sandy soil

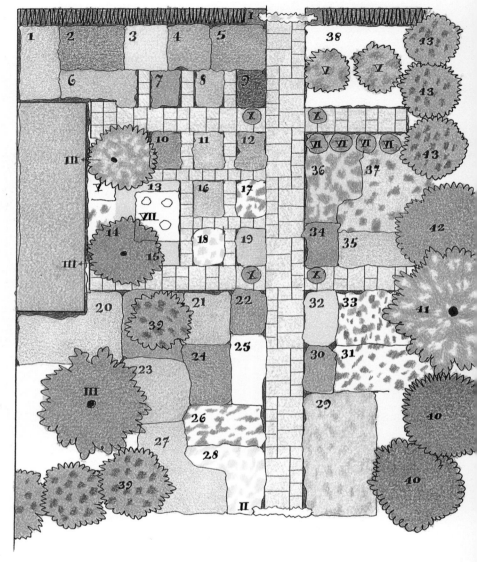

1 *Althaea rosea*, hollyhock

2 *Aconitum napellus*, monkshood

3 *Anethum graveolens*, dill

4 *Allium viviparum*

5 *Nepeta sibirica*, catmint

6 *Artemisia ludoviciana* 'Silver Queen'

7 *Melissa officinalis*, lemon balm

8 *Santolina chamaecyparissias*, lavender cotton

9 *Hyssopus officinalis*, hyssop

10 *Salvia officinalis*, sage

11 *Origanum vulgare*, wild marjoram

12 *Lavandula angustifolia*, lavender

13 *Lysimachia nummularia*, creeping Jenny, and *Ajuga reptans*, bugle

14 *Filipendula hexapetala* and *Lythrum salicaria*, purple loosestrife

15 *Sanguisorba minor*, salad burnet

16 *Allium schoenoprasum*, chives

17 *Asperula odorata*, woodruff

18 *Matricaria recutita*, camomile

19 *Thymus citriodorus* 'Aureus', thyme

20 *Digitalis purpurea*, foxglove

21 *Ruta graveolens*, common rue

22 *Satureja montana*, winter savory

23 *Levisticum officinale*, lovage

24 *Lunaria annua*, honesty

25 *Pulmonaria officinalis*, common lungwort

26 *Tiarella cordifolia*, foam flower

27 *Campanula persicifolia*, peach-leafed campanula

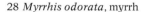

28 *Myrrhis odorata*, myrrh

29 *Angelica archangelica*, angelica

30 *Apium graveolens*, celery

31 *Campanula persicifolia* 'Alba', peach-leafed campanula

32 *Lysimachia nummularia*, creeping Jenny

33 *Fragaria vesca* 'Baron Solemacher', common wild strawberry

34 *Petroselinum crispum*, parsley

35 *Sanguisorba obtusa*, burnet

36 *Alchemilla mollis*, lady's mantle

37 *Monarda didyma* 'Croftway Pink', Oswego tea or sweet bergamot

38 *Convallaria majalis*, lily-of-the-valley

39 flowering currant

40 conifer

41 birch

42 bay

43 currants

I *Rosa* 'New Dawn' over rose archway

II *Rosa* 'Mme Plantier' over rose archway

III pre-existing fruit trees

IV *Clematis montana* 'Rubens' climbing into the birch tree

V Gooseberries on rootstock

VI *Vaccinium myrtillus*, bilberries

X Box (*Buxus*) in pots

the west side because of the various trees there, which is why more shade-loving plants have been incorporated in the largest border. These two gardens cannot be exact copies of each other, firstly because they are different sizes, but also because they do not receive the same amount of sunshine. An attempt towards a similarity has been made, nonetheless, in the choice of blue, white, and yellow as colours for the flowers, and by following the same general layout plan.

A classic kitchen garden (see page 140)

While designs for ornamental gardens and their various sub-divisions have changed through the ages, in kitchen gardens there have been variations around only one unshakeable theme going back centuries. Plants are grown in practical rows, or at least in beds, for human consumption and for their cut flowers. A kitchen garden has to be productive rather than beautiful. The example given (page 140) is of an organic kitchen garden of 300m^2 (360sq. yds) with a length of 20m (65ft) and width of 15m (50ft) – of the sort frequently seen in allotments. If your kitchen garden forms a part of your back garden then the garden shed may be elsewhere and the compost heap may have been placed out of visitors' sight somewhere at the end of the garden. Everything in an allotment needs to be close at hand, the reason for the many extra features included in this example.

The garden faces south-east and is protected from the wind on its north-western side by trees and bushes which stand just behind the kitchen garden. Also providing shelter are the large wooden containers at the end of the garden for compost and manure, as well as a shed. Furthermore, partial protection against strong winds on the north-western and north-eastern sides comes from the raspberries, gooseberries, and red-currants, as well as the two plum trees. The 'Opal' plum ensures that the compost and manure heaps are in complete shadow at midday.

Separate beds

The beds are 1.2m (4ft) wide (the first two being 1m (3ft)). The paths in between can just be walked along at their width of 30cm (12in); the central path is 1m (3ft) wide while the path surrounding the garden is 50cm (20in) wide. The 240 x 150cm (8ft x 5ft) cold frame can be used to propagate seeds and younger plants. It is a good idea to label and number the corners of the beds clearly to help you remember annual crop rotation. General composting for all soils, with the exception of clays, is based on 500l (130 US gallons) of matured horse manure and 300l (80 US gallons) of compost + 40kg (9lbs) of potash fertilizer per 100m^2 (120sq. yds). Leguminous plants and root crops should only be given the potash.

An informal garden (see page 141)

An attempt has been made to make this fairly long garden (diagram on page 141) appear shorter and wider by the method of planting. The garden has been divided up into three areas: the first, next to the mulberry tree, belongs to the patio on the south side; the second is

Planting

A box border behind the cottage

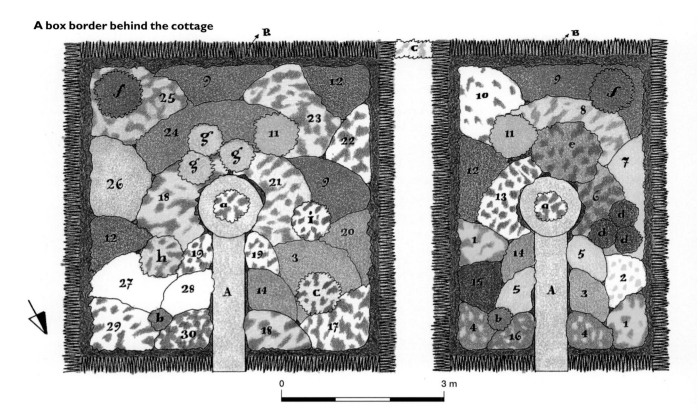

A paving with old brick

B box hedge

C rose-covered archway using *Rosa* 'New Dawn'

a *Rosa* 'Iceberg' on rootstock, x 2

b *Buxus sempervirens*, x 2, box topiary sphere

c *Potentilla fruticosa* 'Eastleigh Cream'

d *Caryopteris clandonensis* 'Heavenly Blue', x 3

e *Ceanothus thyrsiflorus* x *repens*

f *Hedera colchica* 'Arborescens', x 2, ivy

g *Euonymus fortunei* 'Vegetus', x 3, spindle

h *Corylopsis pauciflora*

i *Fothergilla major*

1 *Euphorbia martinii*, 2 beds, euphorbia

2 *Rudbeckia purpurea* 'White Lustre', coneflowers

3 *Ruta graveolens* 'Jackman's Blue', 2 beds, rue

4 *Epimedium perralderianum* 'Frohnleiten', 2 beds, barrenwort

5 *Salvia officinalis* 'Icterina', 2 beds, sage

6 *Lavandula angustifolia* 'Hidcote Blue', lavender

7 *Helianthella quinquenervis*

8 *Phlomis russeliana*

9 *Aconitum napellus*, 3 beds, monkshood

10 *Phlox paniculata* 'White Admiral', phlox

11 *Humulus lupulus* 'Aureus', 2 beds, golden hop

12 *Anchusa italica* 'Dropmore', 3 beds, anchusa, deep-blue flowers

13 *Salvia froskahlei*, sage-like

14 *Geranium platypetalum*, 2 beds, cranesbill

15 *Catananche coerulea*, cupid's dart, blue

16 *Alchemilla mollis*, lady's mantle

17 *Polygonatum officinale*, Solomon's seal

18 *Epimedium versicolor* 'Sulphuricum', 2 beds, barrenwort

19 *Houttuynia cordata* 'Plena', 2 beds

20 *Meconopsis betonicifolia*, Himalayan blue poppy

21 *Aconitum septentrionale* 'Ivorne', white monkshood

22 *Cimicifuga ramosa* 'Atropurpurea', bugbane

23 *Nepeta goviana*, species of catmint

24 *Matteuccia struthiopteris*, ostrich feather fern

25 *Symphytum grandiflorum*, comfrey

26 *Hosta* 'Krossa Regal', plantain lily

27 *Anemone hybrida* 'Honorine Jobert', anemone

28 *Geranium sanguineum* 'Alba', cranesbill

29 *Euphorbia amugdaloides* ssp. *robbiae*, euphorbia

30 *Aruncus aethusifolius*

where the garden narrows next to the ornamental pear tree; the third is under the bower or "roof" of plane trees where the shrubbery forms a link with the wooded garden beyond (the partition is a wire fence covered in ivy). The whole concept has a light-hearted character based along fluid lines. The three areas are separated by evergreen bushes in order to maintain the same image in winter. Ivy grows up against wire netting on the eastern side where there are empty spaces in the conifer hedge, and this hides the waste disposal bins behind. A wood-chip path runs through the western border in the garden's mid-section to make access to both sides of the border easier, and is curved to fit in with the garden's total concept. Old, broad bricks have been cut in two to produce a Roman-brick effect, and a row of these edges the lawn. A space 50cm (20in) wide, necessary for maintenance, has been left clear next to the conifer hedging.

An amusing design using lettuce: a kind of carpet bed.

A shaded herb garden (see page 142)

Most herbs need sun but, fortunately, there are a few which are suited to the shade which could be an idea if you have a shady spot left over in your garden. This little garden (page 142) measures up at 4.4m x 4.4m (14ft x 14ft) and has paths 60cm (24in) wide. Box or privet can be used here for hedging since beech does not fare so well out of the sun. As well as some well-known kitchen herbs, some old-fashioned flowering plants have been added too, just as in the monastery gardens of the Middle Ages.

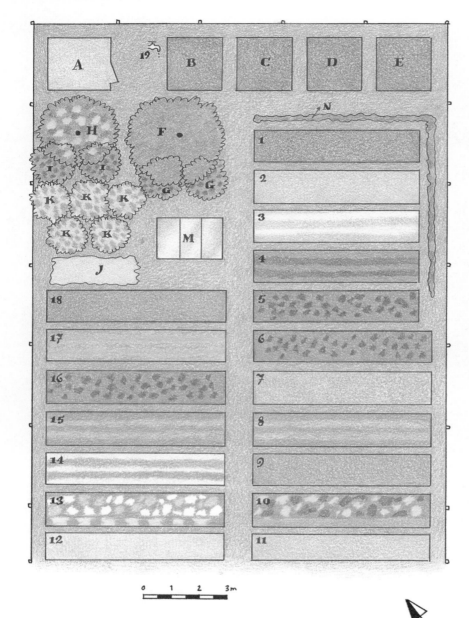

13 chrysanthemums and celeriac
14 peas, later autumn leeks
15 broad beans and potatoes
16 strawberries and lettuce
17 carrots and onions
18 tomatoes

A patio next to house (brickpaving)
B patio at back of garden (concrete tiling and brick paving)
C lawn

I *Platanus acerifolia* used as a plane-tree bower
II *Pyrus salicifolia* 'Pendula', ornamental pear tree
III *Morus alba*, white mulberry

a *Abelia grandiflora*
b *Buddleia davidii* 'Black Knight', butterfly bush
c *Lavatera* 'Barnsley'
d *Pieris japonica*
e *Viburnum bodnantense* 'Dawn'
f *Rhododendron aberconwayi* and *R. yakushimanum*
g *Hydrangea macrophylla* 'Nigra', hydrangea
h *Taxus baccata* 'Fastigiata', yew
i *Taxus baccata* 'Repandens', yew
j *Hibiscus syriacus* 'Mauve Queen', hibiscus
k *Callicarpa bodinieri* var. *giraldii*
l *Rubus thibetanus* 'Silver Fern', ornamental bramble
m *Buddleia davidii* 'Pink Delight', butterfly bush
n *Amelanchier lamarckii*, juneberry
o *Hydrangea paniculata* 'Unique', hydrangea
p *Clethra alnifolia*, sweet pepper bush
q *Ceanothus thyrsiflorus* 'Repens'
r *Ficus carica*, fig
s *Hedera helix*, ivy
t *Clematis* 'Hagley Hybrid'

A classic kitchen garden

a shed
b sieved compost
c manure heap
d mixing container
e compost heap
f 'Opal'
g red-currant (x 2)
h 'Reine Victoria'
i red-currant (x 2)
k gooseberry bushes (x 5)
l seed onions
m cold frame
n raspberries

1 red cabbage
2 garden peas, later endives
3 garden peas, later finocchio (vegetable fennel)
4 early beetroots, later Kenya beans
5 strawberries and lettuce
6 strawberries and lettuce
7 late-cropping potatoes
8 broad beans and early-cropping potatoes
9 peas, later French beans
10 chrysanthemums and carrots
11 oxheart cabbage, later curly kale
12 oxheart cabbage, later Brussels sprouts

An informal garden

1 *Hosta fortunei* 'Hyacintha', plantain lily

2 *Astrantia major*, masterwort

3 *Pachysandra terminalis* 'Youngii'

4 *Anemone tomentosa* 'Robustissima', anemone

5 *Eupatorium rugosum*, hemp agrimony

6 *Liriope muscari*

7 *Verbena bonariensis*, species of verbena

8 *Salvia sclarea*, clary

9 *Euphorbia martinii*

10 *Agastache foeniculum*

11 *Heuchera micrantha* 'Palace Purple'

12 *Helleborus argutifolius*, Corsican Christmas rose

13 *Euphorbia amygdaloides* 'Purpurea'

14 *Alchemilla mollis*, lady's mantle

15 *Pulmonaria longifolia*, common lungwort

16 *Tellima grandiflora*

17 *Lysimachia punctata*, loosestrife

18 *Anemone vitifolia* 'Honorine Jobert'

19 *Aster novae-angliae* 'Andenken an Alma Pötschke', Michaelmas daisy

20 *Hosta plantaginea* 'Grandiflora', plantain lily

21 *Polygonum amplexicaule*, knotweed-like

22 *Cephalaria gigantea*

23 *Macleaya cordata*, plume poppy

24 *Foeniculum vulgare* 'Bronze Giant', bronze fennel

25 *Polygonum campanulatum*, knotweed-like

26 *Bergenia cordifolia*, saxifrage

27 *Dicentra formosa*, broken heart

28 *Helianthus salicifolius*

29 *Tradescantia andersoniana* 'Leonora', trinity flower

30 *Origanum laevigatum* 'Herrenhausen', marjoram

31 *Cimicifuga ramosa* 'Atropurpurea', bugbane

32 *Astilbe pumila*, perennial spiraea

33 *Geranium phaeum*, cranesbill

34 *Aster divaricatus* and *Euphorbia amygdaloides* 'Purpurea'

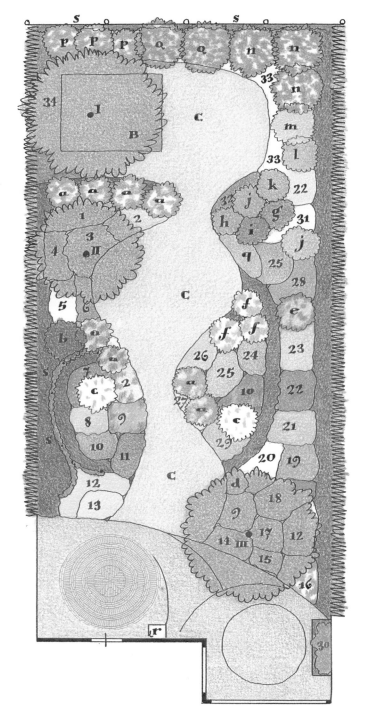

A shaded herb garden

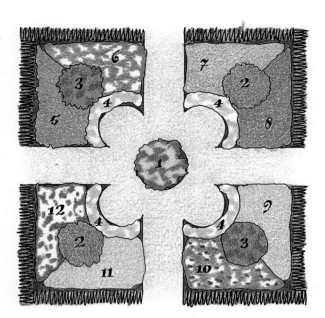

0   1 m

1 *Angelica archangelica*, angelica

2 *Campanula latifolia* 'Macrantha', giant bellflower

3 *Aquilegia vulgaris*, granny's bonnet

4 *Asperula odorata*, woodruff

5 *Apium graveolens*, celery

6 *Convallaria majalis*, lily-of-the-valley

7 *Viola odorata*, sweet violet

8 *Petroselinum crispum*, parsley

9 *Allium schoenoprasum*, chives

10 *Fragaria vesca*, common wild strawberry

11 *Dicentra spectabilis*, broken heart

12 *Anthriscus cerefolium*, chervil

Photographers

L. Geers, Dongen: pages 18, 19, 20 right, 111 right

M. Kurpershoek, Amsterdam: title page, pages 5, 7, 8, 11, 13, 14, 15, 16, 26, 30, 31 below, 41 below, 47, 49, 50, 51, 52 left, 58, 60, 62, 63, 64 below, 67, 68 left, 73, 74, 75, 76, 78, 80, 81, 83, 89, 92 above, 93, 98, 100, 101 left, 102, 103 right, 106 above, 113, 114, 115, 116 above, 121 below, 123, 125, 127, 129, 130, 131 above, 131

G. Otter, IJsselstein: pages 9, 12, 27, 45, 52 right, 56, 61, 64 above, 65, 66, 68 right, 69, 77, 79, 84, 86, 87, 91, 96, 99, 101 right, 103 left, 104, 107 above, 110, 117, 120, 121 above, 131 below, 139

P. Schut, Haarlem: pages 6, 10, 17, 19, 20 left, 21, 22, 23, 24, 28, 29, 31 above, 33, 34, 36, 37, 39 above, 40, 41 above, 42, 43, 44, 53, 54, 55, 57, 59, 70, 71, 72, 82, 85, 90, 92 below, 94, 95, 97, 105, 106 below, 107 below, 108, 109, 111, 112, 116 below, 118, 119, 126, 128, 132, 135, 136

N. Vermeulen, Groningen: page 124

The publisher and the author would very much like to thank the following persons for all the help they so willingly gave to producing this book.

Mevr. D. Paulus van Pauwvliet, Oosterhout; Mevr. W. van Tilburg, Oosterhout; Mevr. T. Froeling, Oosterhout; Mevr. D. Dekker, Dongen; Mevr. P. van Bergen, Oosteind; Mevr. I. van Engelen, Dongen; Mevr. J. van der Heyden, Dongen; the K. Gerris family, Dongenvaart; the De Man family; Mevr. G. Kavelaars-van Meer, Zevenbergschen Hoek; the G.J.W. de Haan family, Dongen; Mevr. A. à Campo, Dongen.

Index